NIXON'S ELUSIVE TOTALITY

NIXON'S ELUSIVE TOTALITY

IT DEPENDS ON WHO WRITES THE HISTORY

LEE HUEBNER

Published by Miniver Press, LLC, McLean Virginia

ISBN: 978-1-939282-62-0

Library of Congress Cataloging-in-Publication Data

Summary: A former speechwriter for Richard Nixon takes a new look at one of the most controversial leaders in U.S. history. Huebner argues that both Nixon's critics and his defenders have missed out on this full story, as he traces in some detail the roots of the man's complexity, from his difficult childhood through his final Watergate crisis in 1973 and 1974, during which, as Nixon himself later put it, "I did myself in."

"Today is a day for his family, his friends and his nation to remember President Nixon's life in its totality."

PRESIDENT BILL CLINTON AT RICHARD NIXON'S MEMORIAL SERVICE. APRIL 27, 1994.

TABLE OF CONTENTS

PREFACE

WHY STUDY NIXON?

This book grows out of nine years of personal interaction with Richard Nixon, including five years as a White House speechwriter. It also reflects some 25 years of teaching a college course focused on Nixon—first at Northwestern University and then at the George Washington University. The book, like the course, responds to the initial question I have been asking my students through the years, "Why Study Nixon?"

The question reflects my own curiosity (shared by many others) as to why this course should consistently be over-enrolled even a half century after Nixon's resignation as President? It's as if I had signed up when I was in college for a class about William Howard Taft!

The students' responses emphasize contradictions in what they have heard about Nixon, from parents and grandparents and teachers, journalists and other writers, documentaries and even comedy tv shows. In response, I suggest that those basic contradictions can be found within Nixon himself. In fact, the central lesson of the course, as I see it, is that people are complicated, politics are complicated, and life is complicated. And we should thus avoid being trapped by stereotypes and over-simplifications, not only in considering historical matters but also in our approach to contemporary matters. My hope, in short, is that the university course (like this book) will underscore the importance of critical thinking—a readiness to explore, analyze and evaluate a representative range of relevant information.

New student impressions of Nixon—while still focused on the concept of "controversy" —have evolved through the years. The dominant words in their introductory submissions some thirty years ago were "I am not a crook" and, occasionally, "China." Later, words such as "paranoid and "corrupt" appeared more frequently, along with politically related observations ranging from "Nixon paved the way for Trump" to "Trump makes Nixon look better and better!" Most recently, terms like "EPA" and "environment" have joined the list—reflecting a new generation's intense concerns about ecology—and a recognition that it was Nixon who proclaimed the first Earth Day, created the Environmental Policy Administration, and promoted the initial Clean Air and Clean Water Acts.

This writer participated in drafting the president's public statements on many of these ecological issues—in part because I was the youngest person on the writing staff and environmental concerns were then relatively new to the political arena. But there is a great deal in Nixon's own history and that of some key advisors that testifies to their deep interest in such matters. (He liked to recall boyhood dreams of visiting the alluring beauties of nearby mountain ranges but never having the opportunity to do so.) Of course, political considerations entered the picture at a time when leading Democrats such as Senators Edmund Muskie and Gaylord Nelson emphasized environmental concerns.

But student interest in such matters may also, at least potentially, reflect a new public curiosity about what Nixon did beyond foreign policy during his five and a half years in office. And while some Nixon alumni are still absorbed in defending Nixon against Watergate-related critiques, others have been re-exploring other elements of the President's record. My former White House colleague, John Price, summed it up in the title of his recent book entitled *Nixon, The Last Liberal Republican,* emphasizing the long-honored (although now-forsaken) progressive Republican traditions with which Nixon also sometimes identified. Such complexities provide another rewarding answer to the question "Why Study Nixon?"

There are many fascinating aspects to the Nixon story. He was a dominant figure on the national scene from his first Congressional election victory in 1946 though his resignation from the Presidency in 1974—and even afterward, as he published some ten books during the final two decades of his life. His public career spanned the whole of the Cold War—from "Yalta to Yeltsin." Meg Greenfield of *The Washington Post* famously once mused that she was part of a "Nixon generation," one that lasted a half-century. She was too young to remember a time when Nixon was not in the nation's headlines, and too old to foresee a time in which he would not still be prominent. During his career, he became one of only two people, along with FDR, to have appeared five times on national election tickets—three times as a presidential candidate and twice as the vice-presidential nominee.

Nixon was not necessarily a successful figure throughout this period—and in fact he was often at his most effective when he was fighting back after serious reversals. And his was, indeed, a roller-coaster career, beginning with his emergence as a controversial anti-communist crusader in the 1940s and then continuing, during his first Congressional term, with his leadership role in the era-defining Alger Hiss case. His ascent continued with his election to the U.S. Senate in 1950 and then his nomination as Dwight Eisenhower's vice-presidential running-mate in 1952. That success was quickly followed by his near dismissal from the ticket amid false allegations of financial scandal, and then his recovery following his "Checkers speech"—the very first nationally televised political address. He lost the 1960 presidential race against John F. Kennedy by an extremely narrow margin, but he did not contest the result, although many of his followers and some independent journalists felt he had cause to do so. That election was quickly followed by the success of his self-defining book, *Six Crises*, and then by his significant 1962 loss to Pat Brown for the governorship of California. His response to that defeat was his defiant "last press conference" in which he declared, "you won't have Nixon to kick around anymore!" It ushered in what he came to call his "wilderness years"—which then ended with his narrow presidential victory in 1968. His tumultuous first term in the White House was climaxed with his historic visits to both China and the Soviet Union in 1972—and then by his record-setting re-election victory, as he won with 49 states and 60.7% of the popular vote, only .4 points behind Lyndon Johnson's 1964 landslide.

But within months, a highly popular bumper-sticker was exclaiming: "Don't blame me. I'm from Massachusetts," (the only state Nixon did not carry in 1972)—amid the unfolding explosions of the Watergate Scandal.

* * *

"Awful but Wonderful"

The complexities of the Watergate White House were particularly apparent to me on my last day of working there in February of 1974. As usual, there was a departure photo opportunity with the President in the Oval Office. Often, in my experience over the years, a chance to observe how uncomfortable Nixon could be with casual small talk. I witnessed again his oft-repeated presentation of a go-away souvenir. ("It's a candy dish. You can give to your wife—or your girlfriend. …Or use it as an ashtray!") I interposed my thanks for the five-year experience by saying, even more awkwardly, "Well, it's been great fun!" which was clearly not a word an astonished Nixon expected to hear at the very moment that the Watergate scandal was about to enter its worst stages. "Fun????" he exclaimed with astonishment. And then, quickly recovering, he quietly continued: "Well, yes, I know what you mean. It' s just that it's so sad for me to think of all our young people, and the hopes they had when they first came here."

And then, wrapping up on a more personal note: "So, you're moving to New York?"

Pause. "An Awful City!"

And then a slightly longer pause before the experienced politician continued: "Awful. But Wonderful!!"

"'Awful. But Wonderful.' Not a bad title to use in a White House memoir," I thought as I left the Oval Office in early 1974.

CHAPTER ONE

A SOLEMN CHILD

Among the many hundreds of insightful books that have been written about Nixon's life, the best account of his childhood was written by an unusual British author, Jonathan Aiken. His biography, *Nixon: A Life* (1993), has long been out of print, but it is still valued for its insights into the early shaping of Nixon's views on life and politics. Aitken was a young British politician when he first met Nixon, and Nixon cooperated with Aitken's biography project by sharing family documents and memories and by opening contacts with other people who had observed Nixon's early years (and many who had shared in his later years, including this writer).

Aitken's highly promising political career had been derailed by financial scandals, some prison time and then a religious conversion, after which he became a respected prison counselor and later an Anglican priest. He also wrote about a story that paralleled his own, that of Charles Colson, the first Nixon counselor to be imprisoned in the wake of the Watergate affair. (Colson later acknowledged that he had often appealed to Nixon's "dark side," the President's "dark" and "light" sides having been a frequent discussion topic among his White House staff.) Later, Colson also became a religious leader, while founding an advocacy organization called the

Prison Fellowship. He was among those who actively encouraged Jonathan Aitken's spiritual renewal.

So, what did Aitken—and others more recently—have to say about Nixon's early family life?

One key was the sharply contrasting nature of his parents. His mother, Hannah, was a deeply religious Quaker, a pacifist idealist, and a profoundly private woman—reserved even in expressing emotion within her family. Nixon's father, Frank, was often quite the opposite in nature, contentious and combative, inside and outside the family. "I loved my parents in different ways," was Nixon's later comment. The family faced economic struggles, and Richard himself had to put in long workdays in the grocery store and gasoline station that his father had started in Whittier, California after the family's lemon ranch had failed in Yorba Linda. Both communities at the time were newly emerging amid the ranches and fruit groves east and south of Los Angeles.

In his farewell speech to his staff on his last day as President, Nixon described his mother as "a saint,"—observing a bit resentfully that "no one will ever write a book about my mother," a not so hidden reference to a recent book about Rose Kennedy, matriarch of the Kennedy family. Nixon then went on to describe his father as someone who many would have called "a little man, a common man," but arguing instead that his father was "a great man because he did his job." President Bill Clinton's eulogy at Richard Nixon's funeral would recall the first line of Nixon's own memoir: "I was born in a house my father built."

The family challenges that may have most deeply shaped young Richard's life, however, were the deaths of two of his four brothers—his young brother Arthur, who died suddenly at the age of 7, when Richard was 12, and his oldest brother Harold, who passed away after a long battle with tuberculosis when Richard was 20. Observers have suggested that two family losses left Nixon with something of a survivor's guilt complex, and a sense that he had to be "three sons in one" to help make up for their loss.

He began to do so in high school and then at Whittier College, enrolling there when it became clear that he could not afford the full costs of attending Harvard University, despite having been offered a tuition grant. His disappointment regarding his lost opportunity may have played into his later anti-establishment hostility to many things that were Harvard-related. (This writer later wondered aloud to colleagues just what it really implied when Nixon introduced me to others as "one of my Harvard Men." On the other hand, his first two appointments as President-elect in 1968 were Harvard Professors Daniel Patrick Moynihan and Henry Kissinger).

His record at Whittier was marked not only by strong academic grades, but also by considerable success in inter-scholastic debate competitions and student government elections. (The key to his student election success, he said, was his "radical" proposal to allow dancing on this conservative Quaker campus.) An observer suggested that "he willed himself to be popular" (then and later) despite his continuing image among many teachers and fellow students as "a solemn child," and a "Gloomy Gus" with an "iron butt." Later in life, he would describe himself as someone who was not a "buddy-buddy" kind of person. Others would conclude that he was decidedly uncomfortable in "the world of drinks and jokes," someone who often felt that he needed to "prepare a face to meet the faces that we meet," in the words of T. S. Eliot. Despite his shyness, Nixon was also regarded as an intelligent leader who was respected by a range of classmates.

He also began to date regularly a lively woman named Ola Florence Welch—a relationship that some, including Nixon himself, believed would lead to their marriage. Welch, whose sister once described Nixon as "a real pill," felt that she never understood her boyfriend, despite their active college social life. An early bond was what they both recalled later as a highly excruciating moment when his role called for him to kiss her (awkwardly) in a high school drama—to an uproarious student eruption of catcalls and derisive laughter. They dated regularly in the early 1930s. But the relationship ended with a letter she wrote to Nixon in his second year at the Duke University Law School, announcing her plans to marry someone else. Nixon's response included a pained request that she be sure to invite him to her wedding.

Nixon's "trust issues" seem to have been confirmed and compounded by the experience. He found a way, in Aitken's words, of "burying the hurt within himself," and moving on. (He failed to recognize Welch at a school reunion in 1970.)

The story fed into a diagnosis which was expressed by Henry Kissinger when he asked, late in Nixon's career, "Can you imagine what this man could have been had somebody loved him? He would have been a great man had somebody loved him." When asked, after his retirement, about his apparent loneliness, Nixon's shared his view that the essence of great leaders he had known or read about was that they were "lonely men."

Nixon's intelligence and energy compensated, again and again, for his decidedly introverted personality. The key question, then and now, is why such a thoroughly introverted young man chose to enter such a decidedly extroverted profession.

Among Nixon's first college accomplishments at Whittier College was organizing a student association called the "Orthogonians" (best translated as "Square Shooters"), identified by their opposition to the privileged "establishment" students, the Franklins. The sensibilities involved are best captured by pages from the school's yearbook in which photos of the tieless and coatless "Orthogonians" are sharply contrasted with the formally dressed "Franklins." It is an early reminder of Nixon's later efforts to attract a culturally congruent political base, which he came to call his "Silent Majority."

Another long-remembered element of his college career was his role as an enthusiastic member of the football squad, mostly as a willing "tackling dummy" in team practices. He hoped his pronounced readiness to be knocked over and jump to his feet again could help compensate for his relatively small size and notable physical awkwardness. Regarding the latter point, Jonathan Aitken remarked on first meeting Nixon about his poor hand-eye coordination—then evident in his clumsiness with sugar tongs. And others have attributed to this same condition the fact that his infamous White House taping system had to be voice-activated, unlike the similar system of his predecessor Lyndon Johnson, that could be turned off and on selectively by hand-manipulating a hidden button.

The most important element in Nixon's football experience was the role of the Whittier football coach, a person of Native American descent, Wallace Newman, know widely as "Chief." Nixon came to see him as the strong and steady father figure on whom he could consistently rely. Others, then and since, have noted how Nixon often sought out serious, older men as confidantes and companions. The strong memory of Chief Newman's influence also would play a role during Nixon's presidential years, when he surprised many critics by embracing with marked enthusiasm a major reform of federal policy regarding Native Americans.

Another major influence on Nixon's development was his maternal grandmother, Almira Milhous. She gave young Richard a portrait of Abraham Lincoln that hung in his bedroom throughout his formative years, accompanied by a poem by Henry Wadsworth Longfellow.

> Lives of great men all remind us
> We can make our lives sublime.
> And departing leave behind us
> Footprints on the sands of time.

These words were reflected in Nixon's persistent, personal ambitions—as he thought about the likely historical impact of his own footprints. But perhaps most telling in accounting for Nixon's later career were four lines from another Longfellow poem, which also accompanied Almira's bedside gift.

> The heights by great men reached and kept
> Were not attained by sudden flight,
> But they, while their companions slept,
> Were toiling upward in the night.

"Toiling upward in the night" in order to leave "footprints on the sands of time" well summarize what became Nixon's personal philosophy. To "toil upward" became his lifetime passion. And toward what end? This was less evident. As his speechwriters came to recognize, he loved to speak somewhat abstractly about "the lift of a driving dream." And, for him, that dream ultimately reflected another element of his Quaker heritage—to build "an enduring structure of peace."

Soon after leaving the presidency, Richard Nixon found a memorable way to describe his outlook in a conversation with his former aide, Ken Clawson, as reported in Aitken's biography.

"What starts the process really are the laughs and slights and sneers when you are a kid. Sometimes it's because you are poor or Irish or Jewish or Catholic—or ugly—or simply that you are skinny. But if you are reasonably intelligent and if your anger is deep enough and strong enough, you learn that you can change those attitudes by excellence, by personal gut performance, while those who have everything are sitting on their fat butts."

His comment expresses vividly his commitment to "toiling upward"—but with additional emphasis on the dark character of the struggle, calling upon what he would also call "four o'clock in the morning courage." His comments indicate, as well, that a key motivating factor can be a leader's sense that his "companions," and competitors, are not only asleep but are also unworthy.

Hard work—driven by deep anger and personal resentment. These are useful words to use in summarizing much of the Nixon story. This appraisal is echoed in a recent book (2024) by Daniel Silliman, News Editor at the publication *Christianity Today*. Entitled *One Lost Soul, Richard Nixon's Search for Salvation,* the book is a probing theological exploration of Nixon's serious religious thinking—or, in fact, of its relative absence in his life. His Quaker family's pattern of daily prayer and regular church attendance, with four services on Sundays, as well as his later organization of regular White House Sunday worship services, have become popular reference points in describing Nixon's religious orientation. But a sense of religious trust in God's grace did not become a part of his thinking—or so Silliman strongly argues. Instead, an emphasis on salvation by "works" became Nixon's key to a meaningful life, the harder the work the better, even if the work never brought for him the sense of fulfillment and satisfaction that is often the hope of a religious quest.

Striking in this regard is Nixon's own retrospective acknowledgement that even his most important successes were accompanied by a sense of disappointment. "A strange melancholy came over me," he said regarding his record-setting victory in 1972, perhaps explained by the fact that he no longer had a major uphill battle ahead of him, around which he could organize his energies and his resentments.

His close speech writing aide, Bill Safire, summed it up this way. "He could be a good loser. But he was a sore winner."

* * *

Back to California

Nixon ranked high in his graduating Duke Law School class—and made an effort to stay on the East Coast: "where the action is," as he would later say. He applied for a position with the FBI, but it did not come through, and he later learned it had been eliminated. He returned to Whittier, where he joined a small legal practice. Professionally, he became known as an empathic counselor to clients, including divorcing young couples. This writer remembers how Nixon pondered emotionally on the plight of "those poor kids," as he to pointed to the many overnight marriage chapels during an impromptu automobile tour of Las Vegas between campaign appearances there in 1964.

Nixon joined a local theater group, where he met a young teacher, Patricia Ryan. (She didn't like her legal name, Thelma.) Highly self-reliant and energetic, she was a Nevada native who had been orphaned during her teenage years. Nixon told her on their first date that he intended to marry her, but she resisted: "I thought he was nuts or something!" He courted her with typical determination for two years, even driving her into Los Angles for dates with other men. They married in 1940, and their daughters, Tricia and Julie, were born in 1946 and 1948.

World War II took the Nixons to Washington, where his job with the Office of Price Administration provoked a lifelong disdain for bewildering bureaucracies. Despite his Quaker mother's pacifist objections and his own issues with motion sickness, he enlisted in the Navy.

The Navy years found Nixon serving as a chief supply officer on a small Pacific Island, a rare moment when he could feel he was "one of the boys." His well-managed "Nick's Snack Shack" became a popular social center. His other major pastime, playing poker, helped net him some $5,000, which he would later invest in his first campaign for public office.

He was invited upon returning to the U.S to become the Republican candidate in his district's 1946 Congressional election. His highly favored opponent was a liberal five-term House member, Jerry Voorhis. Nixon's energetic campaign stole the spotlight from a preoccupied and disorganized Voorhis, while capitalizing on a nationwide postwar sense that it was time to support the "outs" against the "ins." Throughout that campaign, Nixon employed a "negative campaigning" strategy—focusing on the threat posed by the still-lively radical elements in the Democrats' New Deal coalition—including "softness" on communism. Nixon's performance in five debates against Voorhis helped him to a 56% victory in November, as Republicans captured the House of Representatives for the first time since 1928.

Nixon critics would later spotlight one factor to explain his upset victory, his presumed effort to link Voorhis to communist endorsers. The controversy stemmed from the existence of two Political Action Committees with some overlapping views and memberships. One of the PACs had endorsed Voorhis (as Nixon would emphasize); the other, which had active Communist supporters—did not. Voters did not grasp this distinction, and while Nixon claimed that he had not explicitly misstated the facts, neither did he try to clarify them. Most historians have since concluded that the PAC confusion was <u>not</u> a central factor in Nixon's strong victory. And it is also worth noting that Nixon was reelected two years later with the endorsement of both major parties.

Nonetheless, the consequent charge that Nixon was a "red-baiting, dirty campaigner" would follow him forever, gaining additional visibility following his bitterly negative campaign for the U.S. Senate in 1950. But, even in 1946, it began to fuel the important rise of ardent "Nixon haters," whose animosity would be reenforced by Nixon's central role, less than two years later, in exposing Alger Hiss—an establishment favorite—as a one-time communist spy.

CHAPTER TWO

SUDDENLY: A NATIONAL SPOTLIGHT

It began with a warm welcome from the new Republican House Speaker Joseph Martin, who granted Nixon's request to become a member of the House Education and Labor Committee. There, he would demonstrate his moderate policy preferences, while becoming a friend of another freshman legislator, John F. Kennedy of Massachusetts. Martin would also include Nixon as the only newcomer to join a congressional delegation touring postwar Europe. The trip helped to shape Nixon's understanding that the communist threat required a creative internationalist response, rather than the domestic isolationism that was ardently embraced by some traditional Republican leaders such as Ohio Senator Robert Taft. Nixon's enthusiasm in this regard would lead to his strong support of the Democratic administration's Marshall Plan to aid the recovery of postwar Europe, and then of the NATO alliance and other responses to the emerging Cold War challenges.

Martin also proposed that Nixon join the controversial House Un-American Affairs Committee (HUAC), acknowledging his hope that Nixon might help "smarten it up." The Committee had emerged in the late 1930s as a far right-wing voice in the battle against New Deal liberalism—and alleged domestic communism. Jonathan Aitken's Nixon biography pulled no punches in describing HUAC as "a motley collection of unsound mediocrities and uncontrollable bigots."

Nixon was understandably cautious about the potentially tainting HUAC assignment, but he finally accepted it. He may even have seen it as an opportunity for him to shine by way of contrast with his fellow members. And the contrast was clear at the start as he diligently avoided some of HUAC'S more extravagant and reckless entanglements, such as its hearings about alleged communists in Hollywood.

It fell to Nixon, however, to become the face of the anti-communist movement in the most explosive telling of HUAC's dramas—the charge of serious Communist involvement by leading New Deal Democrat and popular internationalist Alger Hiss. Washington rumors about Hiss turned into explicit charges in 1948, made chiefly by Whittaker Chambers, a *Time* magazine editor, who told the Committee that he had shared in Hiss's communist involvements in the 1930s.

In response, Hiss gracefully defended himself, persuading the Committee and most of the public of his innocence. Most Committee members were ready to drop the matter. Even Nixon's wife and mother warned him at this point to avoid the Hiss case—as did John Foster Dulles, the leading foreign policy voice in the Republican Party. But Nixon had spotted inconsistencies between the Chambers and Hiss testimonies that seemed to warrant further exploration.

The central question for Nixon became "Who is Lying?" A highly relevant piece of evidence, he suspected, was Hiss's consistent testimony that he "never knew a man by the name of Chambers." But what if Chambers had been using a different name in his communist days?

As it turned out, he had.

Hiss would eventually acknowledge that he had known Chambers by the name of "George Crosley." But his careful, earlier effort to avoid a misstatement under oath continued to create major doubts in Nixon's mind. Nixon's suspicions were heightened as Chambers impressively recalled obscure details about Hiss's life and family. One example was an unusual "prothonotary warbler" that the bird-watcher Hiss had once talked about—and proudly mentioned again when Nixon asked him about it. Another such detail that Chambers recalled was the "sassy Ford roadster" that Hiss once had driven. Words like these became grist for the public gossip mill as the Hiss hearings progressed in August of 1948. Radio and newsreel coverage of the mounting drama seized daily public attention that summer (television was still too new). And at the center of it all was 35-year-old Richard Nixon.

Later observers have come to emphasize other elements in Nixon's focus on the case, including the fact that the polished, confident and articulate Hiss was the ultimate establishment "Franklin"—while the mumbling and rumpled Chambers was at the "Orthogonian" end of the cultural spectrum. And Hiss had further infuriated Nixon when the Californian asked about his educational background at Harvard. Hiss's lofty response: "And yours I believe was Whittier?"

The hearings raised public skepticism about Hiss, but the central issue concerning his active communist history remained unresolved until the fall, when an over-confident Hiss sought to restore his earlier reputation by suing Chambers for his presumably false accusations. Chambers response was to recover long hidden microfilms of 1930's documents that Hiss had allegedly lifted from government files for transmittal to the Soviet Union. They became publicly known as the "Pumpkin Papers," as Chambers had hidden them briefly in a pumpkin on his Maryland farm. Their emergence brought Nixon back from a brief Caribbean vacation, which he could afford to take as he was running unopposed. He posed for useful photo opportunities as he examined the films, dramatically posing with a pointless magnifying glass. His key consideration was to keep the issue alive in the hope that a bipartisan consensus would persuade the Justice Department to bring the case to court after the Presidential election in November.

Along the way that fall, Nixon suffered a heart-stopping moment when a Kodak employee announced that the microfilm used in recording the incriminating 1930s documents had been manufactured only recently.

That erroneous finding was quickly corrected, but Chambers' initial reaction to the news was to purchase and ingest rat poison.

Chambers recovered to become a leading conservative commentator. His influential book, *Witness,* in 1952, would tell of his conversions both toward and away from communism. (Nixon even reviewed the book for the *Saturday Review of Literature*.) Meanwhile, the microfilmed documents which Chambers had preserved became a central focal point, first in the court of public opinion, where their mere existence swung attitudes strongly against Hiss, and then at two Hiss perjury trials in 1949. The first ended with a hung jury and the second with a perjury conviction, which led to Hiss's imprisonment.

But another key part of the story had just begun.

The Hiss Speech

Nixon had just passed his 37th birthday when the Hiss guilty verdict came down in January of 1950. That outcome, greeted with some astonishment at the time, has over the years been substantiated through impressive scholarship—including the highly detailed work of Allen Weinstein, *Perjury: The Hiss-Chambers Case (1978)*. Also telling have been revelations from Moscow files following the fall of the Soviet Union regarding that country's communist spy networks of an earlier era. Nonetheless, the will to believe in Hiss persisted in some quarters, emerging most strongly at moments when Nixon himself seemed weakest—for example, his "last press conference" following his 1962 California defeat, when Hiss was featured as a guest television commentator. And similarly, Hiss re-emerged during the Watergate affair, when an implausible rumor was revived that Nixon and the anti-Hiss forces had "built" what they then described as Hiss's wife's typewriter, on which the Chambers papers had allegedly been fabricated.

The Hiss verdict was announced on January 20, 1950—his prison sentence came down on January 25. Nixon immediately asked for a special order to address the House of Representatives that Thursday morning, January 26. The speech had been elaborately prepared, long-awaited and eagerly trumpeted. It was delivered to a packed and attentive Chamber. It extended well beyond its allotted one hour and was greeted at the end with a standing ovation. Nixon himself considered it the most important speech he had yet given.

In the address, he effectively launched a new chapter in American politics, one that would shape public conversation for much of the next decade. The speech also can be seen as launching a new passage in Nixon's own psychological life, as he would consistently blame later controversies on the fact that the liberal establishment, including much of the national press, never forgave him for his role in the Hiss case. He, in similar fashion, would often refer to his establishment enemies as "Hiss types." In the Watergate period, this explanation would become something of an obsession, as he instructed his White House associates to read his account of the matter in his book, *Six Crises.* Charles Colson claimed he had read it "sixteen times".)

Nixon's 1950 speech in the House of Representatives begins by recounting in what now seems like excruciating detail just how the Hiss case had emerged, with a strong emphasis on the legal precision with which he and others had pursued the matter. His point was not to claim personal credit for exposing Hiss: many already agreed with former President Herbert Hoover that the conviction of Alger Hiss was "due to your patience and persistence alone."

But many others found it easier to identify Nixon with HUAC's "rude and ruthless" reputation, and to think of Hiss still as "the darling of the liberal establishment," a symbolic martyr whose downfall might undermine two major causes in which Hiss had played an active role: the domestic accomplishments of the New Deal and the internationalist embrace of the United Nations.

As mentioned above, it is difficult to recapture, many decades later, the polarizing sense of national division that the Hiss case engendered. This writer recalls how social friends once mentioned, admiringly, that they had attended Hiss's funeral in 1996, and how deeply shocked they were to learn of my own Nixon connections. It seemed, briefly, that we were again speaking across a once un-spannable canyon.

In this context, it is worth remembering that a sense of profound polarization is not new to the American scene. It can even be reassuring to recall how the country eventually managed to navigate extreme emotional passages such as the Civil War, the campaigns of the Ku Klux Klan (not only in the South but in northern states as well), the runaway emotions engendered by the Red Scare after World War I, the anti FDR tirades of Father Coughlin and Huey Long in the 1930s, and the later extremist appeals of candidates such as George Wallace. The anti-communist frenzy that immediately followed Nixon's 1950 address provides an instructive addition to this list, although Nixon's first major goal in preparing the speech was decisively to separate himself—and the Hiss case—from the extremist emotions engendered by the controversy. He was determined to establish, clearly, that, as President Eisenhower later put the matter, "You got Hiss, and you got him fairly."

The second, central purpose of the 1950 speech, however, was to argue that the significance of the case went well beyond what had happened to one man, and that it also involved matters of global historical significance. He subtitled the speech *"A Lesson for the American People."*

The urgency of the message grew out of the march of recent history. The 1948 Hiss headlines had followed by only a few weeks the Communist blockade of Berlin and the Communist takeover in Czechoslovakia. In 1949 came the fall of China and first Soviet atomic bomb. Within days of the speech, as the Nixon team worked to circulate the text massively across the country, news would break about the passage of U.S. atomic secrets to the communist East, spotlighting Klaus Fuchs' exposure in Great Britain and the Rosenberg spy case in the U.S. For a while, in the context of a newly developing Cold War, everything seemed to be going wrong from a Western standpoint. The time had come, Nixon declared, "not only to halt but to roll back the red tide which to date has swept everything before it."

The speech quickly was used as a key campaign document, not only to help launch Nixon's 1950 bid for a U.S. Senate seat, but also as a call to arms for the Republican party as it worked to broaden support after some 20 years of Democratic dominance. To this partisan end, Nixon would make the most of President Truman's dismissal of the Hiss case as a "red herring" and Secretary of State Dean Acheson's early declaration that he would "not turn my back" on Hiss, an old family friend. After Adlai Stevenson emerged as the new national Democratic leader, Nixon enjoyed attacking the party of "Adlai, Alger and Acheson." The "coddling" of communism by Democratic leaders would become a familiar Republican trope.

As it happened, it took just three weeks after the Nixon House speech for that partisan strategy to take an unwanted, and, in retrospect, a grim turn. An obscure freshman Senator from Wisconsin decided to use the Nixon speech as the basis for his Lincoln's Birthday speech in Wheeling, West Virginia. Joseph McCarthy, who had originally planned to talk to that local audience about housing policy, not only borrowed Nixon's anticommunist contentions but he also, and at some length, repeated the actual language of the Nixon House speech. And, as he read it, he also changed it. Where Nixon had kept score by citing some 800 million people who were now living under Communism, the Wisconsin Senator read out 80 billion. And where Nixon counted 540 million people still "on our side," McCarthy told the Wheeling audience that the figure was "about 500 thousand."

More than that, he also added a fateful sentence which would unleash a national nightmare: 'I have here in my hand a list of 205 names that were known to the Secretary of State as being members of the communist party and who nevertheless are still working and shaping policy in the State Department."

The charge, it is now clear, was ridiculous. The "list" never existed. But the rhetorical torrent that followed, not only from McCarthy's skeptical critics on one side but also from many Republican enablers on the other, badly tainted Nixon, who tried both to exploit, and eventually, to contain the consequences. Adlai Stevenson would pithily sum up an emerging view that Nixon was "McCarthy in a white collar," and *Washington Post* cartoonist Herbert Block (known by the moniker "Herblock") would draw a heavily bearded Nixon in company with McCarthy, often holding a tar bucket and crawling out of a sewer.

Independent of McCarthy's "hijacking" of the speech, within days hundreds of thousands of reprints of the actual Nixon text were circulating across the country, not only to long lists of California voters, but also to more than 7000 US newspapers editors, many of whom reprinted it. Nixon proudly cited "a number of editorials that appeared as a result of that mailing," and additional requests for copies were being fulfilled well into April.

Meanwhile, Nixon's U.S. Senate campaign itself quickly evolved into a different, darker story—one that in the end had a more damaging impact on Nixon's image among liberals than the Hiss case itself, in that helped to solidify in many eyes the McCarthy connection. His California opponent was liberal Congresswoman Helen Gahagan Douglas, a former actress. Nixon was tutored in the race by his campaign manager, Murray Chotiner, a veteran Republican operative who had advised on Nixon's controversial 1946 campaign. Chotiner's appetite for conflict and controversy had been summed up in his assessment that the purpose of a political campaign was not "to defeat" but rather to "destroy"an opponent. Nixon came to agree.

As a result, their 1950 crusade was long remembered not only because it sent Nixon to the Senate with 59 percent of the vote, the largest Senate margin in the country that year, but also because of its vitriolic excesses. Best remembered was the charge that Douglas was the "pink lady" who was "pink right down to her underwear" (a line that was borrowed from Douglas's earlier Democratic primary opponent). Hundreds of thousands of attack documents were circulated on pink paper—claiming that Douglas had voted many hundreds of times with New York's communist-leaning Congressman—Vito Marcantonio. The claim was misleading in it the array of similar votes included myriad automatic, routine and non-partisan questions. Democrats all across the country would remember and endlessly recount such Nixon excesses as something more problematic than mere "campaign tactics." Over time, the dark implications became part of the Nixon image for many, reenforced by Douglas's memorable counterattacks on "Tricky Dick."

Even before he entered the Vice Presidency, American grade school students were entertaining one another by pointing to Nixon's picture and asking: "Would you buy a used car from this man?"

The stakes —and the criticisms—heightened significantly when Nixon became General Eisenhower's running mate at the 1952 presidential election.

Nixon had not yet met Eisenhower when he was selected for that role, largely on the recommendation of New York Governor and two-time Republican presidential nominee Thomas Dewey. Nixon's relative moderation and his internationalism were one part of his appeal. But his slashing, burning campaign reputation was also seen by some as a particular plus, given the General's non-political, war-hero image. Nixon could do the "dirty work," someone said. And he did, opening the campaign with bitter attacks on the incumbent Democratic administration—its alleged softness on Communism and its tolerance of corruption.

For the Republicans, as the Fall season opened, Nixon was quickly deemed to be Ike's "Hatchet Man." For the Democrats he would quickly emerge as a particularly weak link in the Republican campaign operation.

And then, a little dog named Checkers became a national celebrity.

CHAPTER THREE

THE CHECKERS SPEECH

On September 23, 1952, the GOP vice presidential candidate opened a new era in political communication. A careless—and in the end, unsupportable—attack alleged that Nixon had abused, for personal purposes, a political expense fund set up by California supporters. His response was the first American speech to be televised for a national audience, watched or heard by some 60 million people. It was the largest audience ever assembled.

A 1999 poll of leading communication scholars ranked the address as the sixth most important American speech of the 20th century, close behind the soaring addresses of Martin Luther King, Jr., John F. Kennedy, and Franklin Delano Roosevelt.

The speech salvaged Nixon's career, plucking a last-second success from the jaws of abject humiliation. It also foreshadowed the emergence of a new conservative populism in America, emphasizing social and cultural "identity" more than economic issues. The trend would ultimately help end the domination of the New Deal Democratic coalition.

* * *

Nixon began his speech by explaining the purposes of his expense fund, as well as its record of prudent, transparent management. At the end he moved from defense to offense, describing the charges as retribution for his anti-communist crusading, and delivering a blistering attack on the Truman administration.

But it was the middle passages of the speech, laying out his family's financial circumstances in what Nixon described as "unprecedented" detail, that galvanized an instantaneous turnaround in popular opinion. It was the largest such polling swing ever. Later labeled a "financial striptease," it concluded with words that are still among his best-remembered:

> "That's what we have. And that's what we owe. It isn't very much. But Pat and I have the satisfaction that every dime that we have got is honestly ours....I should say this, that Pat doesn't have a mink coat. But she does have a respectable Republican cloth coat, and I always tell her she would look good in anything.
>
> One other thing I probably should tell you, because if I don't, they will probably be saying this about me, too. We did get something, a gift, after the election.... You know what it was? It was a little cocker spaniel dog ... black and white, spotted, and our little girl Tricia, the six-year-old, named it Checkers. And you know, the kids, like all kids, loved the dog, and I just want to say this, right now, that regardless of what they say about it, we're going to keep it."

The word "Checkers" would come to define the message in public memory, but it was the word "they"—emphasized resentfully by Nixon as he spoke about his omni-present enemies—that captured its bitter tone. Often compared to Franklin Roosevelt's "little dog Fala" speech only six years earlier, its delivery sharply differed from FDR's supremely confident and bemused style. The contrast came to characterize public comparisons of the two leaders, often to Nixon's disadvantage.

* * *

When Whittaker Chambers published *Witness* he recalled the recent Hiss affair as an epic social conflict. On one side, he said, were "the plain men and women of the nation … bowed together under the common weight of life." Against them were "those who affected to act, think and speak for them … the 'best' people … the enlightened and the powerful." The division had long been used by Democrats to rally farmers and laborers against business-oriented Republicans. But Chambers' formulation recast the division, moving beyond pocketbook controversies to focus on "values" and "lifestyles." His book heralded a new strain of grassroots conservatism and Nixon seized the rhetorical opportunity. *Witness* had topped the *New York Times* best seller list for three months in the summer of 1952. Its outlook, and even some of its language, made its way into Nixon's September address.

Nixon would always and only refer to it as "The Fund Speech," resenting the trivializing "Checkers" label. Yet even supporters would remember it less as a spirited defense of his "Fund" and more as an earnest expression of middle American lifestyles.

Nixon, then 39, later described the speech preparation process as the "hardest," "sharpest" and "most scarring" experience of his young life. His salvation, as he saw it, would lie with "millions of Americans," watching and listening in homes across the land. "God must love the common people; He made so many of them," Chambers had written in *Witness*, quoting Lincoln. Nixon's speech would highlight the same quotation.

Scripps-Howard columnist Robert Ruark, saw the point immediately. "The sophisticates…sneer," he wrote just after the address, "but this came closer to humanizing the Republican Party than anything that has happened in my memory.… Tuesday night the nation saw a little man, squirming his way out of a dilemma, and laying bare his most private hopes, fears, and liabilities. This time the common man was a Republican, for a change.… [one who] suddenly placed the burden of old-style Republican aloofness on the Democrats."

The speech positioned Nixon as the ultimate underdog in an unprecedented drama. And yet the charges against him were entirely unproven. Nixon's later, Watergate-logged history, is often read back into the 1952 context, feeding a casual assumption that the Fund allegations must have had something to them. But neither journalistic investigation in that day nor historical research since have substantiated those charges of impropriety. Private funds to cover travel and mailing expenses had been a widely accepted practice. And Nixon's supporters had taken pains to immunize his Fund from criticism.

As its organizer, Dana Smith, told prospective donors a year earlier, the "pool" of contributors to the Fund would include only people "who have supported Dick from the start," preventing "second guessers" from making "any claim on the senator's interest." Contributions were limited to a maximum of $500, so that no one could think he was "entitled to special favors." The money, finally totaling $18,000, went into a regularly audited trust account. Rather than exemplifying the unhealthy influence of money in politics, the Nixon fund can plausibly be seen as an early attempt to respond to that problem, as his biographer Roger Morris has suggested.

When Nixon was first asked about the Fund charges on Sunday, September 14, both he and his aides took the matter too casually. But three other factors quickly allowed the story to get out of control. The first was the inaccuracy of some journalists, exemplified by the pace-setting *New York Post* headline: "Secret Rich Men's Trust Fund Keeps Nixon in Style Far Beyond his Salary."

A second factor was the aggressiveness of political opponents, especially Democratic Party chairman Stephen Mitchell, who called immediately for Nixon's resignation. As one historian has put it, the Democrats' handling of the Fund crisis was "criminally stupid." Interestingly, the one prominent Democrat who did not join in the frenzy was presidential nominee Adlai Stevenson, partly because his own private expense funds were so similar to Nixon's.

But the third and perhaps most important factor in sustaining the Fund controversy was the ambivalent reaction from General Eisenhower and his entourage.

Nixon's oratorical fervor had escalated as the Fall election approached. In a telling response to his "hatchet-man" label he had shouted: "If the record itself smears, let it smear. If the dry rot of corruption and communism ...can only be chopped out with a hatchet, then let's call for a hatchet." Later even he would describe his rhetoric as "unconscious overreacting" to opposition attacks.

But Eisenhower and his advisors were uncomfortable even with the excesses of normal campaign rhetoric, and Nixon's style deepened their discomfort. Many among them were remarkably ready to entertain the fund-related rumors, worried that they might be "the tip of the iceberg." Some were put off by his social awkwardness. Others worried that his language would link the campaign too closely to the unhappy rise of McCarthyism. Their campaign, after all, had been shaped as a moral crusade against "politics as usual." Ike's comment that his campaign must be "as clean as a hound's tooth" was regarded by many as a warning to Nixon.

When journalists on the Eisenhower train voted (rather unprofessionally) by a count of 40 to 2 for Nixon's removal from the ticket, and when letters and telegrams began to run 3 to 1 against Nixon, the pressure on the General intensified. It culminated in an anti-Nixon editorial in the influential *New York Herald Tribune*, a strongly Republican newspaper.

The hope—and expectation—of Eisenhower's advisors was that Nixon would simply withdraw from the ticket. California's arch-conservative senior senator, William Knowland, the GOP Senate leader, was asked to join Eisenhower's entourage and to stand by as a substitute running-mate. And Nixon seriously considered resigning. He would spare himself an enormous agony—and avoid being remembered as the man who dragged down Eisenhower.

But two considerations argued the other way. First, resigning would give credence to the charges and hand his enemies a victory. The thought of yielding deeply offended him—and it outraged his wife. Pat Nixon had opposed his accepting the vice-presidential nomination, but her fierce sense of pride now came into play. Nixon must not "crawl," she urged in an anguished two a.m. conversation after they first learned of the devastating *Herald-Tribune* editorial.

Meanwhile, there were strong political arguments for hanging tough. While staying in the race meant risking blame for Ike's defeat, leaving the ticket would by no means ensure success; early polls showed a close contest. Nixon's resignation would offend conservatives and party regulars and could drive away swing voters. And Nixon would still be the scapegoat.

Nixon decided to fight. He would agree, of course, to do the General's bidding, but he would not "draw up my own death warrant."

Remarkably, it was only on the night of Sunday, September 21st, that the two men spoke by telephone. Ike endorsed the idea of a televised explanation, an idea that had been championed by Robert Humphreys, media guru for the Republican National Committee. But the General refused to commit himself to a quick up or down decision, even after such an appeal.

Nixon reacted angrily. "This thing has got to be decided at the earliest possible time," he lectured the five-star general. "There comes a time in matters like these when you have to shit or get off the pot!"

In his 1961 book *Six Crises*, Nixon rephrased his retort to read, "you've got to fish or cut bait," but in his 1978 memoirs he acknowledged the earthier language. It expressed not only his mounting frustration but also his sense, as he put it to Eisenhower, that "the great trouble here is the indecision." Eisenhower's stance, on the other hand, clarified Nixon's challenge. As he later remembered: "Now everything was up to me."

The challenge was daunting. Thomas Dewey warned Nixon that a mildly favorable response to a televised explanation would not be enough—perhaps a 90 percent approval ratio might be required. And it soon became clear, as Humphreys had argued, that neither an interview program nor free time from the networks would do the job. Only by paying $75,000 for a half hour of prime time could Nixon maximize the audience and control the format.

It is remarkable, in retrospect, that so many tactical media decisions were then made so well and so quickly. They included not only paying for a primetime television broadcast, but avoiding a coveted Monday night slot (after *I Love Lucy*) and selecting a Tuesday availability (following Milton Berle's popular comedy show), allowing enough to time to build an audience without waiting too long and dissipating the tension. The campaign refused to disclaim rumors that Nixon would be quitting—further heightening suspense. They eliminated any studio audience (even press and staff watched from another room), and finally, they selected as a stage setting "a GI bedroom den," a comfortable middle-American set, including a desk, a bookcase and an armchair for Pat Nixon.

Underlying these decisions was a concept still new to the television era, although it had characterized Franklin Roosevelt's fireside chats on radio. For the first time, a national television audience would share directly in a living room to living room encounter. It would be Nixon, alone, with the people. The reporters and the politicians—his own staff and Eisenhower's—would all watch on television. And none of them would know what he was going to say.

* * *

Six days after the Fund charges first appeared, Nixon's west coast train tour had ended in Portland, Oregon. He flew to Los Angeles, where he isolated himself for the next 30 hours at the Ambassador Hotel, sleeping a mere 4 hours and working through a fog of despair that had become a major concern of his associates. Working from preliminary notes made on airplane postcards, he sketched his argument onto legal pads. He incorporated rhetorical elements that had already been "audience tested" on the campaign trail. (Pat's Republican "cloth coat" for example, was a veiled reference to the so-called "mink-coat scandals" of the Truman years).

He decided against using a full manuscript—it would forfeit the "spark of spontaneity" he valued so highly. He was finishing the fifth and final page of his second outline on Tuesday afternoon, when a bizarre development intervened; Dewey phoned, relaying Eisenhower's request that Nixon end the speech by submitting his resignation from the ticket. Devastated by the request, Nixon stood his ground. "Just tell them that I haven't the slightest idea what I am going to do," he responded when Dewey pressed him. "And if they want to find out they'd better listen to the broadcast."

There was no time now for a third outline, no time to memorize or to reconsider his path. Grabbing his five pages of notes, he left for the old El Capitan theater twenty minutes away in Hollywood. When Ted Rogers, his television advisor, asked how he would close, Nixon replied, "I don't know…" Three minutes before airtime, he told his wife, "I just don't think I can go through with this." "Of course you can," she responded, taking his hand and leading him to the set.

The last page of his scribbled notes read: "The decision must be made by Nat'l Committee. I will abide by their decision. You help them —let them know either way…" That formulation meant defying Eisenhower's request.

In the end he mistimed his closing comments and never gave an address for contacting the Republican National Committee—the only group with the power to change the party nominees. At the moment, the error seemed fatal. "I loused it up, and I'm sorry. It was a flop" was the first thing he said after going off the air, throwing his notes to the floor and burying his head in the stage draperies. But even this slip turned to his advantage as supporters, unsure of where to send their responses, sent multiple copies in many directions.

By one count, there were some 4 million responses to the speech—virtually all of them pro-Nixon. The National Committee alone reported 300,000 letters and telegrams signed by a million people. The count ran 350 to 1 in Nixon's favor.

The address not only touched a responsive nerve in the body politic. It seemed to open a national tear duct: Nixon's first hint that the speech had succeeded, he said, came when he noticed tears in the eyes of the cameramen. Eisenhower's wife Mamie, watching in Ohio, wept as the speech ended. In California, the man who removed Nixon's makeup told him, "There's never been a broadcast like it before." Ted Rogers reported that the theater switchboard was lit up "like a Christmas tree." "Thousands were in tears of emotion," wrote the *Los Angeles Examiner*, describing the effect as a "wildfire." A cowboy in Missoula, Montana, handed a $100 bill to a Nixon associate with the comment, "That's the best speech I ever heard." Back in Cleveland, some 15,000 tearful Republicans chanted "We Want Nixon" as they waited for Eisenhower to greet them.

But Eisenhower, who had watched the speech with cool detachment, remained noncommittal. Among other things, he was wondering whether Nixon's call for a full accounting of supplemental income from all of the national candidates would draw attention to the financial success of his own postwar memoir. "I shall make up my mind…as soon as I have had a chance to meet Senator Nixon face-to-face," he concluded, summoning Nixon to meet him the next evening in Wheeling, West Virginia.

When reports of Eisenhower's reaction reached Nixon amid a jubilant celebration back at the Ambassador Hotel, the Californian "blew his stack" as he later put it. "What more can he possibly want from me?" he asked his aide, Murray Chotiner, adding, "I'm not going to crawl on my hands and knees to him." And he dictated a telegram of resignation.

Chotiner tore up the telegram and convinced Nixon to go to Wheeling, provided he could be assured of Eisenhower's support in advance. But this response was interpreted as "insolent" by the General's camp, and for a few hours ragged nerves and wounded pride on both sides threatened to tear the ticket apart again.

In the end, Nixon went to Wheeling, persuaded by his old friend, journalist Bert Andrews, that he need not worry about the outcome: "The broadcast decided that. Eisenhower knows it as well as anyone else. But you must remember who he is…. He is the boss of this outfit." Meanwhile, Eisenhower, impressed by the public reaction, "shrugged and nodded" his assent to a quiet pre-meeting commitment.

By the time Nixon arrived in Wheeling, Eisenhower was "grinning all over," as he climbed aboard Nixon's plane to announce, "You're my boy."

Nixon then told the waiting crowd of two moments in his life when he was proudest to be an American: one was looking down from a Manhattan window while Ike rode by in a postwar victory parade; the other had come that very day when he realized that "all you have got to do in this country of ours is just to tell the people the truth."

* * *

But in fact, the lessons and legacies of the Fund crisis were far more complex than that.

For one thing, a persistent wariness continued to mark the Eisenhower-Nixon relationship. The loyal Republican Old Guard, on the other hand, rose even higher in Nixon's affections. He carefully remembered those who had stood with him that September, including two whose warm letters of support almost leap from the archival box at the Nixon Presidential Library. One was from a young Minnesota lawyer named Warren Burger, whom President Nixon would later make Chief Justice of the Supreme Court. Another came from a junior Michigan Congressman named Gerald Ford.

Meanwhile, Nixon's wary attitudes to the press were intensified. He felt profoundly wronged by what he saw as the malevolence or indifference of many reporters. For him, simply telling the truth had not been enough. Only a direct broadcast appeal over their heads had saved him. When he asked his chief media assistant, James Bassett, about press reactions to the speech, Bassett would mark a new chapter in the life of the candidate—and the country—with his pointed response: "It's not important now."

When columnist Walter Lippman described the Fund speech as a "demeaning experience," he was objecting less to Nixon's emotional appeals than to the fact that a leader like Eisenhower had been forced to count telegrams and telephone calls. "Mob rule," Lippmann called it.

With this new era came new expectations. Though Pat Nixon was shaken by the need to reveal personal financial data, and to appear on the television stage, her husband reconciled himself to living "in a fishbowl." While his proudly private parents cringed as he told of family struggles, their equally reserved son saw such details as a new way to build public rapport. Candidates' families—not to mention their pets—had been only occasionally visible in American politics; After "Checkers," families would become central participants in a new political dramaturgy.

Nixon welcomed the opportunity to identify fully with "ordinary" American lifestyles. Again, it was the Orthgonians against the Franklins. The Checkers speech would persuade millions at the time that he was truly "one of us." (Those three words would later become the title of an influential, revisionist Nixon biography, published in 1991 by Tom Wicker, Washington Editor of the liberal *New York Times.* He later acknowledged the fierce opposition that title encountered, even from his publisher, when he first proposed it.)

Greeted both with enormous empathy and enormous scorn in 1952, the Checkers speech lifted its writer into the first rank of American celebrities. In doing so. it reinforced his confidence that he could rescue himself from even the most perilous of difficulties by appealing directly, through television, to what he would famously come to call his "silent majority." But the experience also left deeper personal wounds than any of Nixon's political crises prior to Watergate. While he buoyantly created an informal club, "The Order of the Hound's Tooth," for those who had shared the ordeal, this was not a success he was ever eager to recall. Pat Nixon simply refused ever to talk about the matter. The bitter legacy would color Nixon's perspectives and influence his judgments for the rest of his career.

It is impossible to read or to watch the Checkers speech six decades later without thinking of a later Nixon, and of later crises. But it is worth trying, nonetheless, to return to this speech much as 60 million Americans came to it in September of 1952, knowing very little about Richard Nixon except that he was a very young man with a very big problem, his back against the wall, making a last-ditch effort to rescue his already embattled career.

CHAPTER FOUR

THE VICE PRESIDENCY

The Vice Presidency raised the stakes both for Nixon and his critics. Was the Presidency next for him?

For Nixon, one step toward that goal was establishing a serious foreign policy reputation, an objective he advanced through extensive international travel. He also cultivated a close relationship with Secretary of State and veteran foreign policy guru, John Foster Dulles. Moreover, as time went by, his rhetoric often became a bit milder than that of the party's hardline cold warriors: for example, he would talk more of "containment" than "confrontation." And he paralleled his foreign policy undertakings with an active interest in domestic affairs that contravened traditional impressions of "do-nothing" Vice Presidencies.

At the same time, anti-Nixon rhetoric also escalated as the 1950s went by. Herblock and others focused not only on his "smear artist" image, but also on his supposed rhetorical inconsistencies—his occasional use of words to blur distinctions and to walk fine lines. One Nixon response was to cancel his home subscription to *The Washington Post*, protecting, he said, his wife and two young daughters from Herblock's grim cartoon images. Pat's response to all the noise was a determined effort to have him retire from public life (which he even promised to do at one point.).

The new Eisenhower administration found itself confronting two public image problems, one caused by McCarthy's continued rampaging, and the other by Stevenson's effort to tie McCarthy to Eisenhower. In response, and at Eisenhower's urging, Nixon agreed to take the lead in repudiating both McCarthy and Stevenson in a national television speech early in 1954. His preparation echoed that of his still-recent Checkers speech" he isolated himself at Washington's Statler Hilton Hotel and prepared a text that clearly called out McCarthy by name. Later, perhaps in an excess of caution, he struck out all of the direct references to the Wisconsin Senator, and instead called more generally for greater discretion in "shooting rats," meaning that anticommunist attackers should be careful not to hit innocent people or scare away other communist rats. He also made an immense round of preliminary, explanatory phone calls, determined that the speech should not surprise or offend his conservative colleagues.

The speech made its intended point. McCarthy realized angrily that it marked a break for him with the Eisenhower administration. The speech can be seen as a first step in the decline of the Senator's support, soon followed by Edward R. Murrow's impactful television denunciation later that month, and then the collapse of the Senator's support during the Spring Army-McCarthy hearings, leading to his censure by the U.S. Senate.

A constant concern with the prospect of renomination in 1956 also haunted Nixon's first Vice Presidential term. Eisenhower's own misgivings were reflected in White House suggestions that Nixon might become Secretary of Defense in a second Eisenhower administration. His renomination was openly challenged by Minnesota Governor Harold Stassen, hoping to spur a moderate GOP revolt, but party leaders, having been carefully courted over the years, stayed with Nixon. The replacement risk became even greater after Eisenhower was sidelined by a severe heart attack in 1955, although that moment offered Nixon a well-managed opportunity to be at his statesmanlike best in stepping into the leadership vacuum—without overstepping! He presided ably over Cabinet meetings, but carefully did not sit in the President's place at the head of the table.

This concern about renomination was also evident in a little-known pre-convention speech in 1956 of which he continued to be particularly proud, delivered on the Pennsylvania campus of Lafayette College, after recent speaking invitations from his two alma maters, Duke and Whittier, had run into campus opposition. The Lafayette address included a proposal that young people should be recruited to work on extended humanitarian projects in the emerging nations of the Third World. The suggestion was warmly welcomed by liberal Minnesota Senator Hubert Humphrey, who would promote it during his Presidential primary campaign against John F. Kennedy. Kennedy took note, and the Peace Corps became a popular success of the Kennedy Presidency. But the idea can also be traced back to Richard Nixon.

The second Eisenhower/Nixon term brought new factors to bear on the question of Nixon's presidential viability in 1960. On the positive side for Nixon was a quasi-heroic image as he calmly withstood the assaults and narrowly escaped serious injury during violent anti-American protests in South America in 1958. He was also dramatically photographed standing up to communism in a different setting during his so-called "Kitchen Debate" with Soviet leader Nikita Khrushchev while touring an American Exhibition in Moscow in 1959.

On the negative side for the Vice President, however, was a public swing against Republican leadership in general, triggered by a serious economic recession and the consequent Democrat triumph in the Congressional elections of 1958. Added to this sense of reversing GOP fortunes was a public impression that the Eisenhower administration had grown old and weary and that the Soviet Union was on the rise—having launched Sputnik, the first space satellite, in 1957, thus arguably taking the lead in the military missile race.

The 1958 midterm outcome was a crushing blow for Nixon. He had again campaigned "up and down the ticket and up and down the country" in the preceding weeks. Now deeply disheartened as he considered the new political landscape, he almost canceled his post-election trip to Great Britain. Instead, he once again responded to deep disappointment by taking on a new challenge, which culminated in what he later said was his best speech ever, a statesmanlike address in late November at London's English-Speaking Union. He would later urge supporters to ponder the speech; he would suggest it as a model to his White House speechwriters. Highlighting former Prime Minister's William Pitt's assurance that England had "saved herself through her exertions and would save Europe by her example," it proved a soaring reminder of the lasting power of ideas in international life. The British found it inspiring as they entered their post-colonial era, and it worked to re-enforce Nixon's diplomatic credentials at home.

Eisenhower's uncertainties about Nixon continued, meanwhile, to hover over the Vice President's future, accentuated when Ike was asked as the election approached whether he could name a major policy contribution by Nixon during his administration. Ike's response, presumably intended as a humorous one, was: "Well, if you give me a week I might think of one." It was regarded as a blow to the Vice President's hopes, although perhaps offset when Ike chose to campaign actively with Nixon in the closing days before the election.

A Tied Election

The 1960 presidential election would be one of the most closely contested and perhaps most carefully remembered in later years, in part because of the breakthrough success of The *Making of the President, 1960*, Theodore H. White's behind-the-scenes account of the two clashing campaigns.

The election result itself was a virtual tie. John F. Kennedy was officially confirmed to have won by 112, 827 votes—0.17 percent—giving him an electoral college majority of 303 to 219. The close popular margin focused attention on two states, Texas, home to Kennedy's running-mate Lyndon Johnson, and Illinois, where Chicago, ruled by Mayor Richard Daley, became a central battleground. In both states, powerful political machines had often been accused of miscounting votes, and critics would point to voting districts in both jurisdictions where the number of votes cast for Kennedy exceeded the number of people who were registered to vote—although some later voices would try with uncertain success to explain how non-registered voters could still cast legitimate ballots.

The controversies flared briefly in the post-election press (especially in accounts by Earl Mazo of the *New York Herald Tribune*), but they were quickly stilled by the intervention of none other than Richard Nixon. Nixon's close associates—including his wife—encouraged him to challenge the outcome. And some took active steps in that direction. But Nixon, characteristically, framed the potential election crisis in an international context. He suggested that a period of U.S. governmental uncertainty could undermine the global reputation of democratic institutions, at a time when the very concept of democracy was being challenged in many parts of the world.

Nixon also recognized how extremely difficult it would be to reverse enough vote counts --in at least two different states-- to win, while also realizing how the image of a bad loser could seriously damage his future election prospects. He was only 47 years old at the time; Kennedy was 43. If the result confirmed Nixon's lifelong sense that the world was somehow stacked against him, well then, the smart response was to take the setback and launch again on an uphill climb. It was a good moment to prove himself a good loser.

He would demonstrate that quality with particular feeling when he presided over the counting of the electoral vote at the Joint Session of Congress on January 6, 1961, underscoring the greatness of a country where candidates accept election results in the interests of a peaceful transfer of power. He spoke of this cause as "one that is bigger than any man's ambition, greater that an any party."

"It is in that spirit," he concluded, that I declare that "John F. Kennedy has been elected as President of the United States and Lyndon B. Johnson as Vice President."

The standing ovation went on and on—not so much for the victors in this case as for Nixon. And it still should—especially in light of more recent January 6 dramas.

A Battle for the Center

It has been useful for my students to look in depth at the array of competing sentiments as the country moved into a new political era in 1960. It was the first presidential election in which a candidate—in this case, both candidates—had been born in the twentieth century. This did not become a moment of national polarization, however, but rather one in which a wide array of both Democratic and Republican voters re-considered a balanced interplay of competing considerations. The election contest was often described as "a battle for the center."

A majority of the electorate was still Democrat in 1960, identifying with the party of the "little people," the New Deal, and Franklin Roosevelt. Republicans, on the other hand, were still seen by many as the party of Herbert Hoover, Wall Street, and the affluent "country club" world, which made Nixon's contrasting "little man" identification even more useful for him.

Nixon's highly visible foreign travels underscored another viewpoint, prevalent among many Americans, that the Republicans had been a party of strong diplomatic competence. It was a strength on which Nixon doubled down in choosing as his running mate, Henry Cabot Lodge Jr., whose role as Eisenhower's forceful United Nations Ambassador had made him something of a media star in the new 1950s television era. (Coincidentally, Lodge had lost re-election as Massachusetts Senator to none other than John F. Kennedy).

Other GOP rhetoricians would talk insistently about "Democrat Wars," pointing out how both World Wars, as well as the Korean War, had started under Democratic presidents. And, of course, a range of Republicans, led by Nixon among others, had worked hard to characterize the Truman administration and Democrats in general as having been naïve (or "soft") about the communist threat. Nixon would focus, especially during the television debate with JFK, on his opponent's imprecision about just whether or how he would go about defending against Chinese threats to the offshore Taiwanese islands of Quemoy and Matsu. "Communism,

Corruption and Korea" had been the slogan bolstering the Republican return to power in 1952, and its impact was still complicating Democratic prospects in 1960.

Kennedy would try to counter these impressions with his own tough anti-communist rhetoric, working, as many said, to "out-hawk Nixon" by dramatizing the threat of a newly Communist Cuba ("just 90 miles from our shores") and a so-called "missile gap" between the U.S. and the Soviet Union. The latter was an overstretched charge which had been reenforced in the public mind by the Soviet Union's Sputnik launch, combined with the failure in late 1957 of the first US attempt to launch a space satellite, which culminated in the explosion of the Vanguard rocket just two seconds after takeoff. The shooting down of the U-2, an American spy plane, over the Soviet Union in 1960 also played conveniently into a Democratic narrative about how the Republican administration had grown too old and weary to compete effectively against its energetic Communist rivals.

Kennedy also used the age and energy comparison to underscore popular Democratic promises on the domestic front, reenforced by the severe 1958 recession and the accompanying Democratic sweep in the midterm elections. Kennedy's vibrant personal image—widely visible in the new television era—was one of youth and energy, even though his own physical health was problematic. His campaign would also highlight his award-winning Naval heroics in rescuing crew members of PT-109, a torpedo boat he commanded in battle in World War II, as well as the literary success of his book about American Senate heroes called *Profiles in Courage*—written with the important assistance of his close aide, Theodore Sorensen.

It did not take long for the previously little-known junior Massachusetts Senator to overcome suggestions that he was something of a "lightweight" and to become a fascinating new television celebrity. One can recall how informal conversations at the time were suddenly fixing not only on the fluency of his speaking style, but also on his Boston accent when he would talk not only about the new threat coming from "Cub-er," but about the need for greater "vigah" in public leadership.

At the same time, Nixon suffered from the "hangover effects" of his "Tricky Dick" image and his reputation as Eisenhower's "Hatchet" Man." "I do not like thee Doctor Fell / The reason why I cannot tell," was a popular schoolyard chant—applied, of course, to popular uncertainties about Nixon.

Nonetheless, Nixon's 1950s effort to project the image of "A New Nixon" began to have an impact, especially within the GOP. His progress toward the GOP presidential nomination was largely unopposed, and he ensured that outcome by reaching an agreement (called The Fifth Avenue Compact) with the newly emerging progressive Republican hero, New York Governor Nelson Rockefeller. The two men emphasized their agreement on important points—and the only audible counter-voice at the GOP 1960 nominating convention was that of the new conservative hero from Arizona, Barry Goldwater. In this context, Nixon's central campaign challenge would be to battle Kennedy for centrist support.

The Debates

In the end, as Kennedy later said, "it was the debates as much as anything that did it.".

Nixon, to the surprise of some supporters, agreed to join in the first nationally televised Presidential debates in 1960, despite his apparent early lead in the polls and the risk that the relatively unfamiliar Kennedy could benefit most from the massive new television exposure. It may well be that Nixon's earlier television success, especially when he defended himself against corruption charges in the "Checkers" speech, gave him an overconfident sense that television would again be his best friend. Instead, it turned out to be his worst enemy.

Four debates were scheduled, beginning on September 26, 1960, just six weeks before the election.

The first debate seemed to hurt Nixon most in the image contest. Many said that he won the debate on "substance" but lost it on "appearance." There was some evidence that people who listened to the debate on radio thought Nixon had won, unlike the vast majority who watched on television. But this continuing judgment seems to grow out of a crucial failure to recognize that most of those who were listening on radio in 1960 lived in more remote, rural and conservative areas of the county. When I have shown the video of that first debate to my recent students, they are surprised by Nixon's argumentative success, having assumed earlier that he had "lost" the contest.

However, the visible image problem was partly Nixon's own doing. He had lost some eight pounds in recent weeks, following a serious knee injury for which he had briefly been hospitalized. His response was to soldier on with an intensive travel regime, including a strenuous schedule on the very day of this first debate. And, almost unbelievably, he managed to reinjure the knee as he left his car that evening before entering the CBS studio near downtown Chicago. He then refused to use television makeup, further exposing his omnipresent five o'clock shadow. His overlarge shirt collar also accentuated his gaunt appearance. And his light grey suit intensified the problem as it blended into the freshly painted grey backdrop.

He then received what seemed like good advice from his running-mate Lodge: "Erase the assassin image!" Nixon over-complied. His first words, following Kennedy's opening statement, were: "Many of the things Senator Kennedy has said, we can agree with." Throughout the debate, his efforts to seem gracious and cooperative came to seem excessively accommodating to some. Lodge felt that Nixon had "blown it." Nixon's mother called in immediately to ask if he was feeling well. Kennedy's supporters rejoiced in his apparent success.

The second debate came 13 days later. Nixon, in a darker suit and several pounds heavier, quickly projected a much stronger image. His first words, following Kennedy's opening statement, were: "I disagree with Senator Kennedy on three points!"

The debates gave Kennedy visibility—and viability. But they were not what gave him the victory.

There were three other variables that eventually tipped the scales in his favor—the Black vote, support from the so-called solid Democratic

South, and the Roman Catholic vote. Each of them would be a source of considerable frustration for Nixon.

Black voters had had historically supported the Republican Party, going back to its days as "the party of Lincoln." Nixon, a strong civil rights advocate in his vice-presidential years, had a generally favorable reputation among Black voters. But a late campaign development created a last-minute surge of Black support for Kennedy. The Senator, who had actively courted White and even segregationist Southern leaders during the campaign, now decided (after some careful deliberations with his advisors) to phone Coretta Scott King following her husband's arrest during a civil rights demonstration in Atlanta. The action, accompanied by his team's efforts to persuade local authorities to release King, took on important symbolic value. Many Black congregations were urged at church services on the Sunday before the election to support the candidate who had come so visibility to King's support.

King himself later expressed his disappointment that Nixon (with whom he had enjoyed a good relationship) had not similarly offered some gesture of support. Nixon had considered doing so—but carefully backed off rather than jeopardizing his hopes for inroads among southern conservatives. In the end, despite Kennedy's symbolic support for King, many voters in the heavily segregationist Southern states fell back reflexively on old Democratic loyalties. Kennedy wound up "having it both ways"—while Nixon's caution proved costly.

In addition, a significant reason that Kennedy became the first Roman Catholic president was because he won an unusual share of the Roman Catholic vote, and there wasn't much that Nixon could do about that. He realized that anti-Catholic voters could help to offset that Kennedy advantage. But he also knew that any effort to exploit that potential could badly backfire—and he took pains to avoid even mentioning the religious issue in the futile hope that it would simply fade into irrelevance.

Kennedy used a September invitation from the Greater Houston Ministerial Association to present an eloquent defense of the full separation of church and state, and the sympathetic reaction of many non-Catholic voters, determined to demonstrate their own lack of religious bias, wound up working to his benefit. At the same time, as analysts have convincingly pointed out, Kennedy did better than other Democrat candidates had done in Roman Catholic districts across the country.

CHAPTER FIVE

THE 1960S AND "THE NEW NIXON"

Nixon had learned since childhood that the best response to losses was to prepare for future opportunities. The outcome in 1960 had essentially been a tie and he responded by thinking about new ways to stay in the political game. He wrote a book that he called *Six Crises,* reminding the public of the challenges he had confronted in his career to date. And he decided that the best way to prove his political viability was to challenge the incumbent Governor of California, Pat Brown, in the 1962 election.

What that election wound up proving was his political vulnerability. Although Brown was thought to be beatable, Nixon's national reputation did not convert into state and local credentials. He lost by 5 percentage points.

A key reflection in his *Six Crises* book concerned the dangers of a post-crisis let-down moment. His California loss exemplified the point. His long -simmering resentments of the media boiled over as the results became clear. The national public was listening as he addressed the press the next morning:

"As I leave the press, all I can say is this: For 16 years—ever since the Hiss case—you've had a lot of fun attacking me, and I think I've given as good as I've taken.... As I leave you, I want you to know—just think how much you're going to be missing. You won't have Nixon to kick around anymore. Because, gentlemen, this is my last press conference."

The episode constituted "Nixon's political obituary" in the view of many. The damage to his future political prospects had been "irreparable." Ironically, the immediate impact was so shocking that it was remembered a few years later as even worse that it had been. When Democrats looked again at videos of that "last press conference," they decided they would be less useful as 1968 campaign weapons than they had expected them to be.

Nixon's considered reaction was to leave the unhappy scene of his abject defeat—and what he found, in the absence of political engagement, to be a boring and lonely California. He decided to return to the East, "where the action is."

He joined a New York law firm in 1963, and it was then that this writer first met him, as he enthusiastically plunged our visiting team into a deep luncheon discussion of world affairs. He was clearly ready to be "a player" in the 1964 election, but he would carefully avoid a futile presidential quest in the wake of the Kennedy assassination.

Meanwhile, he would prepare for the longer-range future. As he began to build a new staff, he offered this writer a position, and while I did not want to abandon my graduate schoolwork, I accepted his invitation to travel with him for a month as he stumped the country in the 1964 campaign. He understood that, like the Ripon Society organization that I then headed, I did not support the Goldwater candidacy. But he was thinking well beyond the immediate election and already reaching out in all directions as he sought to fashion a broad coalition of eventual support. (His offer to me had been quickly followed by the hiring of the conservative writer, Pat Buchanan, and a bit later, of the journalist Ray Price, who had recently written the unusual LBJ endorsement editorial for the traditionally Republican *New York Herald Tribune*.)

The major ingredient in Nixon's party-rebuilding operation was his many months of grassroots retail campaigning in 1964 and 1966, rallying support within a demoralized party for GOP candidates up and down the ticket. His 1966 effort climaxed in a crucial television speech just hours before the mid-term Congressional election. Searching for a way to share more of the national spotlight, he had baited President Johnson into attacking him (as a "chronic campaigner.") His well-publicized response to LBJ, financed by the Republican National Committee, positioned Nixon as the leading voice of the opposition.

Republicans had nowhere to go but up in 1966, having lost so decisively at all levels in 1964. The party recovered handsomely in 1966—picking up 47 House seats and 4 Senate seats. Sharing importantly in the credit for this comeback was the former Vice President, soon to be labeled by some as "the Comeback Kid." He quickly emerged as the leading Republican presidential prospect in 1968.

* * *

1968: "Nixon's the One"

The year 1968 started badly—and got worse. North Vietnam's Tet Offensive was a major psychological setback for the anti-communist cause (though not finally a military success for Hanoi). Lyndon Johnson, coming to realize how overly optimistic expectations had confounded his war management, stepped back from the struggle and announced he would not seek another Presidential term. Anti-war sentiment burgeoned, kindling not only the presidential bid of Minnesota Senator Eugene McCarthy but also other less temperate protests. And then, a trembling public was further traumatized by the assassinations of Martin Luther King Jr. and Robert F. Kennedy. Democrats settled on Vice President Hubert Humphrey as their presidential nominee at a riot-torn Chicago convention that further undercut national morale.

Meanwhile, still hovering nearby was Richard Nixon, no longer the young 1960 candidate who had never lost an election, but now a two-time loser, remembered most vividly for his "last press conference."

But could he win, even if nominated? Even the grateful party faithful continued to wonder. Nixon, however, had learned a lot from his earlier losses and he would 'play it differently' this time around.

He faced no early competition within the party for the next Presidential nomination. Ronald Reagan had succeeded Barry Goldwater as the conservative hero, but it was only in 1966 that he had triumphed electorally in California. Nor had Governors Nelson Rockefeller of New York nor George Romney of Michigan, once seen as early front-runners, managed to build a strong national following. Nixon could thus focus on his standing with a broad national audience, avoiding divisive, ideological entanglements with Republican rivals.

At the same time, instead of trying, as he did in 1960, to impress the public—and, presumably, himself—with an ardently exhausting schedule, he would set clear campaign priorities. He would avoid needless risks by staying entirely away from one-on-one television interviews, building his pre-convention campaign around public question-and-answer sessions for which the audience and the questions had been selected in advance, in what became known as the Hillsborough strategy, named after the New Hampshire town where it had been initiated. The pre-scripted events were accompanied later by a series of radio addresses, carefully speaking to the issues of the day. The radio format also saved a lot of money, time and energy, eliminating the pressures of speaking to live audiences and nonetheless attracting acceptable press coverage.

Nixon also reached out in new ways to broaden his popular appeal. Though he had been uncomfortable in the world of "drinks and jokes," he worked to round out his super-serious image. He appeared just long enough on the frenzied comedy program *Rowan and Martin's Laugh-In* to shout out its well-honed laugh line: "Sock it to me." He had begun his comeback with a brief, successful appearance on Jack Parr's popular *Tonight Show* in the wake of the 1960 election playing the piano (featuring his own composition) and laughing with Parr as the latter passed along his daughter's wistful comment: "I sure hope that man finds work!"

Nixon would be nominated on the first ballot at the 1968 Republican National Convention, overcoming challenges from Nelson Rockefeller on the left and Ronald Reagan on the right. A key advantage was that his two leading opponents could never join in common cause against him. Both of their constituencies would prefer Nixon's moderation (muddled as it sometimes seemed to them) over the ideological appeals of the opposite side. Even the campaign slogan: "Nixon's the One!" was a way to avoid more substantive claims.

Similarly, his vice-presidential choice, relatively unknown Maryland Governor Spiro Agnew, excited no one. But he seemed at least minimally acceptable to most Republicans, at least initially. Democrats, on the other hand, would quickly make the most of a series of Agnew verbal slips and blunders, airing a television commercial featuring the words "Agnew for Vice President?"—accompanied by twenty seconds of nothing but rising, raucous laughter, and ending with the admonition, "This would be funny if it weren't so serious."

What excited the Republican convention partisans, in the end, was Nixon's return in his acceptance speech to his familiar negative campaigning style. His fierce, fiery rhetoric gave the party a potent theme to rally around: what Nixon painted as the deplorable and dishonorable failures of the Johnson administration at home and abroad.

He minced no words in describing what Americans faced: "Cities enveloped in smoke and flame," the sound of "sirens in the night, and the sight of "Americans dying on distant battlefields.... We see Americans hating each other; fighting each other; killing each other at home." He posed the question: "Did we come all this way for this?" And he underscored his conclusion: The reason for the nightmare was not because the country had failed, but because "her leaders have failed."

The acceptance speech ended, however, on a much gentler, affirmative note, summoning up the face of a child—"an American child...who is everything we ever hoped to be and everything we dare to dream to be.... He sleeps the sleep of childhood, and he dreams the dreams of a child. And yet when he awakens, he awakens to a living nightmare of poverty, neglect and despair." Nixon then contrasts this story with that of another child, one who "hears the train go by at night and dreams of faraway places where he'd like to go.' "This latter child, of course, is Nixon himself, recalling the evolution of his own aspirations—"it seemed like an impossible dream"—and concluding with the declaration, "tonight he stands before you, nominated for President of the United States."

The "face of child" theme had been suggested to Nixon in a letter from a schoolteacher named William Gavin, who was quickly hired onto the candidate's speechwriting team. Also joining the campaign as it entered it later stages—and then dominating the Fall marketing effort —were television executives Frank Shakespeare, Harry Treleavan and Roger Ailes, who would later lead the surge of Fox News as the dominant media voice of American conservatism.

Nixon's acceptance speech not only set the tone for the fall campaign, but it also provided much of the actual script. Fall television ads pounded the message home, highlighting brutal scenes of rioting and warfare, chaos and turmoil. Much of the advertisement soundtrack featured tough, voiceover excerpts from Nixon's convention speech.

All of this would be memorably recalled by Joe McGinnis in his popular book, *The Selling of the Presidency, 1968*, attributing the remarkable Nixon success to Madison Avenue advertising prowess. How else, some of his critics suggested, could a candidate like Nixon have overcome his "immense" handicaps"? McGinnis viewed his book as a warning about the potential power of media manipulation, an argument many people would buy into (and still do).

However, McGinnis's thesis was wrong. As the fall campaign opened, at the end of August, Nixon's led Humphrey 45-29, a margin of 16 points. On election day, the numbers were 43.4 to 42.7 percent, less than a one-point margin. George Wallace, the segregationist Governor of Alabama, polled as high as 21 percent in late September and wound up with 13.5 percent on Election Day.

Nixon's long comeback in the mid-1960s was propelled by a variety of factors, but it is hard to argue, given the fact that his polling lead shrunk that fall by 15 percentage points, that his widely touted fall advertising program was the key factor in his ultimate success.

This writer joined the Nixon campaign staff in New York in September of 1968. Headquarters were in a building that had previously housed the American Bible Society. Somewhat ironically, and sometimes appropriately, we entered each day—to help shape campaign messages—under an archway that was prominently inscribed with the Biblical reminder: "You shall know the Truth and the Truth shall make you Free."

But the truth that increasingly impressed the staff that fall was that the campaign was not going well. Nixon's percentage in the polls was holding even, but it was not going up and Humphrey was gaining steadily, especially as he distanced himself from Johnson by supporting a U.S. bombing halt in Vietnam. At the same time, he emphasized social and economic issues that reminded many Wallace voters of their traditional Democratic roots. And many of them wound up returning to the party fold.

Nixon, of course, had said a great deal about a wide variety of policy matters—but his strenuous, negative campaign focus that fall created a general impression, echoed in the press, that Humphrey was discussing "issues" while Nixon was not. Nixon's campaign staff in New York tried to remind those on the beleaguered campaign plane of the possibilities for correcting the apparent imbalance and then took up that task itself, producing press statements and radio scripts. This writer remembers working in this way on the subject of "Older Americans"—and being told later that it was a rare constituency with whom Nixon's standing may have improved during those weeks.

A more significant New York staff project involved the publication of two large paperback books. One, called *Nixon on the Issues,* was a topic-by-topic compilation of short Nixon statements on many dozens of subjects. The other volume, called *Nixon Speaks Out*, brought together the full texts of Nixon speeches (often radio addresses) about major concerns. I remember a celebration dinner when the books finally emerged with GOP political veteran William Casey, later Nixon's CIA Director. At least, we hoped, our joint project would provide hard evidence that Nixon wasn't running away from tough issues.

Recent accounts of the campaign have often mentioned Nixon's so-called Southern Strategy, attributing to his influence the transformation of the once "Solid" Democratic South into a conservative Republican stronghold. A key step along the way came when Nixon persuaded the segregationist Senator from South Carolina, Strom Thurmond, to support his presidential bid. It was a key factor in blocking Reagan's presidential path that year. Thurmond's quid pro quo was assumed to be a Nixon promise to consult and cooperate with Thurmond --especially on judicial appointments—a sensitive variable in shaping the Federal role regarding school desegregation. It turned out be a false assumption.

Many critics have assumed that Nixon's Southern Strategy was shaped by Kevin Phillips, yet another Republican tactician who worked in the 1968 campaign and then published a book about it, *The Emerging Republican Majority.* The book explained Nixon's 1968 victory by citing his hardline appeals to law and order, implying that they were code words designed to appeal to racist impulses. The Republican Party, Phillips insisted, would never have overcome the towering strengths of the post-New Deal Democratic party unless it made a radical break with its own tolerant traditions. "The whole secret of politics," he wrote, "is knowing who hates who."

Even as most Democrats successfully embraced a range of civil right initiatives, Phillips predicted that the answer for Republicans would be found in the race issue—locking in a solid, race-conscious South and perhaps even picking up animosity-driven Northern votes. And some would say that his sad predictions were not entirely unrealistic.

This writer had an early opportunity to debate with Phillips on a New York television program in 1968, emphasizing the Ripon Society vision of a Republican revival based on a moderate "Suburban Strategy." Phillips found that view naïve. His view of human nature was that, in the long run, racial resentment would be a more dominant influence in shaping American political life than economic concerns.

Nixon's view of politics was different. Sometimes tempted in his angry moments to mirror the cynicism of Phillips and other theorists, he nonetheless had built his career around his ability to choose words carefully, and often subtly, using them to bridge at least some gaps, discover at least some areas of shared interest, and thus build the coalitions on which a thriving democratic polity presumably depended.

To be sure, Nixon clearly did see important political opportunities for Republicans among conservative Southern voters. But he could also, simultaneously, prioritize the pursuit of Northern moderate support.

Nor, in Nixon's mind, would an appeal for conservative support in the South necessarily require him to compromise his Quaker principles regarding race relations, nor his frequently expressed commitment to civil rights progress—to which he had contributed during his years as Vice President. While he argued against the bussing of school children to distant neighborhoods to achieve racial balance, he also endorsed the new civil rights legislation of the mid-sixties. And he also made the argument that the South itself would benefit from a stronger two-party system.

He would emphasize after the Phillips book was published that he had not read it—nor did he share its premises. Phillips agreed; he did not see Nixon as an ally or proponent of his own hard-nosed views. Nor, as we will see, did Nixon's own actions as president reflect a Southern race-oriented agenda, including not only his progressive civil rights record but also his federal court appointments.

Moreover, in analyzing Nixon's 1968 election strategy, one cannot neglect the candidacy of Alabama Governor George Wallace and his famous 1963 appeal: "Segregation now, segregation tomorrow, segregation forever!' With Wallace polling at nearly a quarter of the national popular vote at points (and finally winning 46 Southern state electoral votes), there would have been little point for Nixon to go after hardcore race-based voters (wherever they lived), even if he had wanted to. A moderate, national strategy made much more political sense. In the end, it was that strategy proved successful. But Nixon did not take for granted how slim his margin had been. During Vice President Humphrey's concession call, Nixon consoled the defeated Democratic candidate by saying, "I too know how it feels to lose a close one."

CHAPTER SIX

"WATCH WHAT WE DO AND NOT WHAT WE SAY!"

General public (and press) impressions of Nixon's policy record as President have long been dominated by his transformative impact on the international scene—especially the opening to China and the improvement in relations with the Soviet Union. More recently, a slightly greater awareness has emerged concerning the Nixon domestic record, especially his pioneering engagement with environmental issues.

Student impressions have echoed these patterns in my classes, as they too seem to know relatively little about items in the domestic record. In addressing this topic with them, my approach has been not only to share a general overview of the administration's policy agenda in the early 1970s, but also, just as importantly, to take up the question of why so much happened, and why, then and since, it has received relatively little attention.

The new President's domestic policy agenda was remarkably abundant. But the administration did not see itself as retreading the old familiar FDR and LBJ terrain. It worked to articulate a "Republican Reform" philosophy which placed greater emphasis on marketplace incentives, on stimulating the private sector and maximizing individual choice, on decentralized administration and managerial efficiency.

Regarding a central issue of the time, the administration's approach to school integration in the segregated states of the South emphasized persuasive cooperation over moralistic confrontation—a different sort of "Southern Strategy" from that which is often assigned to the Nixon legacy. And it seemed to pay off. Tom Wicker of *The New York Times* was among the first to quantify the resulting progress; in the first three Nixon years, all Black school districts went from 68 to 18 percent of the total Southern number, while unitary (integrated) districts went from 5 to 90 percent. The Nixon administration meanwhile vastly expanded its inherited civil rights enforcement budget—eight-fold by some accounts. And he tripled the budget for aid to Black colleges and universities.

Environmental concerns were high on the list of domestic initiatives—not only the symbolism of the first Earth Day but also the creation of the Environmental Protection Agency, the establishment of new high standards through Clean Air and Water legislation, and (less noted but of major impact) the Endangered Species Act, which became the basis for a continuing series of protection reforms.

The central internal debate of the first Nixon years concerned the topic of welfare reform, thoroughly discussed in the recent book by John Price, who was deeply involved in the internal debate. It was a struggle in which Nixon, despite considerable conservative opposition, ultimately opted for the Pat Moynihan proposal, renamed the Family Assistance Plan, which in essence supported an annual guaranteed family income.

Importantly, the proposal embraced a national standard, preempting the state-by-state welfare--shopping patterns of the time, while also reenforcing two-parent families rather than encouraging fathers to be absent in order to qualify their families for welfare mother support. It also built on the concept of a negative income tax, which created an incentive to work for additional income, rather than cutting all support when a small amount of earned income appeared.

The proposal's emphasis on providing money—rather than an array of welfare "services"—was at its heart. Nixon liked to call it "workfare," aiming to build family "self-sufficiency," through its financial incentives and its built-in work-or-training requirement. The proposal in the end was too little for many Democrats and too much for many Republicans, although it would later provide a precedent for other successful welfare reform initiatives, including those advanced by President Clinton.

On another front, as the 1972 reelection campaign approached, Nixon, in one of his most important speeches, surprised the world in August of 1971 by closing the "Gold Window," which had previously strapped the value of the dollar to the price of gold. It proved to be one of most impactful of all Nixon initiatives over the long run, replacing the old Bretton Woods system which had under-girded global financial arrangements since the 1940s. He also imposed U.S. wage and price controls, theretofore an impossible option in the eyes of classic free market Republicans. Meanwhile the Nixon White House also became a strong advocate for a "full employment budget," eschewing old balanced budget orthodoxies in favor of running deficits when the economy slowed and tightening spending when inflation threatened. "We are all Keynesians now," Nixon declared in advancing this approach.

In early 1971, Nixon, having seen a popular newspaper column by Ann Landers about the spread of cancer at a time when even using the word "cancer" was still something of a taboo, asked Bill Safire to insert a reference to cancer in his upcoming State of the Union address. It later led to major new Federal spending on this front. The Nixon White House did not invent the term 'War on Cancer," but a *New York Times* editor employed that phrase in a headline over a front-page article about Nixon's address, and it stuck. Many years later, cancer research centers around the country still referred to their founding and expansion as part of "Richard Nixon's War on Cancer."

Yet another reform program that was widely welcomed by the general public, and remembered with special pride by many Nixonites, was opposed by much of the small business community. Known as "OSHA" (the Occupational Health and Safety Administration), it brought government inspectors into workshops and factories all across the country to enforce much-needed new health and safety standards.

One of the most important items in the Nixon budgets were grants that went not to designated Federal programs but rather to state and local governments. The program reflected a central philosophical commitment to governmental decentralization.

Revenue Sharing had been an important focus of my own writing since my Ripon Society days, and it all seemed to climax for me at Independence Hall in Philadelphia as I watched Nixon sign Revenue Sharing into law in late 1972. (The program would later end because of budget tightening during the Reagan administration.) Some of the Revenue Sharing was "general;" some came in the form of "Block Grants," designated for more specific purposes but then administered regionally and locally. For Nixon, the appeal of Revenue Sharing, like that of his proposed Welfare Reform plan, was that it provided money to those who needed it without trying to micromanage its usage.

In his later presidential years, Nixon also broke new ground by embracing a national health insurance proposal, despite conservative fears that "socialized medicine" would inevitably follow. Nixon, again, sought to have it both ways—yes, a federally mandated universal insurance program, but one that would be administered through private health insurance companies.

That measure floundered in Congress largely because of Democratic preferences for a "single payer" system, with the government itself collecting premiums and paying out benefits, as was the case in many other countries. Senator Edward Kennedy, who led much of this opposition, would later acknowledge before he died in 2009 that his decision not to support the Nixon healthcare proposal may have been his greatest mistake in the U.S. Senate. If he had given his backing, the long national struggle over this issue would have been resolved a third of a century earlier, he pointed out. And of course, Kennedy was saying this at the very moment when President Obama was successfully advancing his own national health insurance proposal, incorporating the central Nixon concept of mandated insurance through private companies.

It has become known, of course, as Obamacare, the object of continuing Republican hostility ever since. But, given the disastrous end to the Nixon presidency, the Nixon precedent was not an example that Obama could draw upon in the ensuing debates about Obamacare. This writer, having worked closely on the Nixon administration's health care proposals of 1972 and 1973, has argued that "Nixoncare," had it been passed into law, would have gone beyond Obamacare.

It can thus be said that Nixon embraced two of the major liberal policy concepts of his era—a guaranteed national income and universal health insurance, although neither was to be endorsed by the Congress.

Even a brief listing of Nixon domestic policy positions should also include the following items:

- Unprecedented Federal support for the Arts and Humanities budget.
- Support for the 18-year-old vote.
- Ending the Military Draft and creating the All-Volunteer Military.
- Pioneering presidential support for Affirmative Action in hiring minorities (as part of his Philadelphia Plan).
- Establishing the office of Minority Business Enterprise (a part of his "Black Capitalism" emphasis).
- Supporting Home Rule for the District of Columbia (something he announced on his first day in office.).
- Support for the Equal Rights Amendment.
- Establishing the first Presidential Commission on Population Growth.
- Tying automatic Social Security payments to the rise of inflation.
- A newly active Consumer Protection Office at the White House.
- Creation of the National Postal Corporation (taking the Post Office out of politics).

- Reorganization of the Executive Branch (including the creation of the Office of Management and Budget).
- Creating national standards for pension plans—so that people moving from state to state did not lose pension benefits (the Employee Retirement Income Security Act).
- Nursing Home Reform.
- Key reforms in Federal Native American policy.

Nixon's enthusiasm for this last item, as has been noted, grew partly out his fond memories of his college football coach, 'Chief" Newman. This writer recalls this project with particular interest because he was involved in the final stages of presenting the President's proposals to the public and to the Congress.

Part of the background for this initiative was the new intensity of Native American groups advancing their causes in protests such as the Trail of Broken Promises and the Battle of Wounded Knee. A responsive group of White House staff members, (led by former Ripon Society member "Bobbie" Greene, then 23 years old), had responded to those concerns by fashioning a series of specific reform proposals. They were quickly welcomed by the President, in part because of his memories of "Chief" Newman, and also because the initiatives gave him a forceful way to offset the feeling of some critics that that he had moved too slowly on other minority-related issues.

The proposals focused on opening new opportunities for Native American engagement in the national community, but without terminating the government's commitments to traditional tribal lands and institutions. The proposals thus worked to resolve an ongoing dilemma in federal policymaking regarding Native American issues—honoring deep tribal identifications on the one hand while encouraging broader social engagement on the other. The Nixon administration thus embraced both of what had long seemed to be competing options. It was a widely admired outcome. A group of prominent Native American leaders would soon welcome Nixon's initiative as "the most important breakthrough in minority rights protection since Lincoln's Emancipation Proclamation."

On another important front, despite what some feared in the wake of his Thurmond alliance, Nixon's court appointments generally followed a moderate path. The biggest exception was his Supreme Court nomination of Harold Carswell, a Florida-based federal judge with a highly controversial reputation. His critics could claim, for example, that some 40 percent of his judicial decisions had been reversed. Some also discovered statements from early in his career stridently arguing for racial segregation. The nomination had resulted from a temperamental Nixon reaction to the Senate rejection of his earlier choice of a distinguished conservative South Carolinian judge, Clement Haynsworth. But even the President's strongest supporters, on his own staff and in the Congress, were shocked and embarrassed by the Carswell nomination, although the conservative Nebraska Senator Roman Hruska found a way to support the choice by arguing that "mediocre people" also deserved Supreme Court representation. Nixon's final, successful candidate for the seat turned out to be Harry Blackmun, now remembered as the author of the influential *Roe v. Wade* decision enshrining abortion rights into law.

Why So Much Activity. And Why So Little Recognition?

Why was there so much more domestic policy activity than was anticipated—or is remembered?

Several factors are worth mentioning. To begin with there was a part of Nixon that saw himself as a "reformer," an inheritor of the Teddy Roosevelt GOP tradition, a child of an earnest Quaker family, a protégé of progressive teachers and coaches. In addition, he possessed a significant political impulse to preempt moderate rivals, embracing ideas that had already been suggested from both parties with his presidential support moving them further along their way.

Perhaps most significantly, Nixon also assembled and empowered a wide array of advisors, not only in his Cabinet but also on the White House staff, whose own views appealed to both his own darker and brighter sides. Some of them eventually helped do him in. But others steered him into remarkable reform journeys. Nixon's chief domestic advisor, John Ehrlichman, for example, eventually went to jail for tolerating some aspects of the Watergate coverup. Sadly, he was remembered in his *New York Times* obituary headline precisely for that. But one of his lasting impacts on American life grew out of his deep concern for environmental protection, in which he was centrally supported by some of his own staff members, including John Whitaker, with whom I partnered on several projects.

Another example was Nixon's former law partner and later General Counsel, Leonard Garment. This writer was privileged to work with him on issues such as cultural and educational affairs (areas in which Nixon gave Garment something of a free hand), as well as Native American policy. Garment, in his own memoirs, acknowledged his error in supporting what turned out to be the fatal "Saturday Night Massacre" in October of 1973. He was also the close advisor who, upon leaving the Oval Office one day, shared with this writer his frustrated observation: "Lee, I think that there that there are two different people there and I think I mean that in the clinical sense."

There were a host of other Nixon counselors who were given sufficient "room to roam" to make their own contributions to the parade of domestic initiatives. And, of course, there also were people whose use of their own "room to roam" led to Nixon's downfall.

In addition, as we continue to examine contributions to Nixon's domestic record, there is the fact that that he delighted in surprising and confounding his critics. "These crazies wrote me off," one can almost hear him thinking. "Well, I'll show them how wrong they were!"

Another key factor, as Nixon in his own recollections would proudly emphasize, was his fascination with reading political history. He was encouraged early on by counselor Daniel Patrick Moynihan to read Robert Blake's best-selling biography of 19th Century British Prime Minister Benjamin Disraeli. The central message of the book was Disraeli's view that social progress often came under the leadership of "Tory men with Whig principles." The thought appealed directly to both sides of Nixon's own duality: he too was a Tory (conservative) politician, but one with Whig (i.e. progressive) inclinations. And he often lived up to that influential self-image.

* * *

But why, given all of this domestic policy activity, has it received less recognition than might have been expected? The responsibility begins with Nixon himself.

He famously once declared that "the country does not need a President for domestic policy," suggesting that "the Cabinet can handle all of that." His own time and passions were focused on international concerns.

An additional factor was Nixon's deep caution about the likelihood of making major headway with progressive voters or writers, and the pressing need to maintain his political plausibility with conservatives—a rapidly burgeoning movement within his own party, witness Senator Goldwater's recent successes. One way to do so , he felt, was to "Row with Muffled Oars!" Another was to emphasize conservative values and approaches in his public statements —often using code words like "law and order." Even John Mitchell, his relatively conservative Attorney General (and often his chief political advisor) complained during the unsuccessful gubernatorial campaign of 1962 that Nixon sounded too often as though he were "running for sheriff."

Nonetheless, it bothered Nixon sometimes that there never emerged a compact slogan that would fix his domestic record in the public mind—no "New Deal," no "New Frontier." He asked the writing staff to come up with some effective language in this regard, but the best we ever did was the phrase "'Reform' is the Watchword." It did not catch on.

In the end, the administration's best answer to this communication quandary was summed up by Mitchell himself with his pointed declaration: "Watch what we do and not what we say!"

CHAPTER SEVEN

A LASTING STRUCTURE OF PEACE

Nixon's approach to domestic policy, then, was to welcome a wide array of contributions and then to "row with muffled oars." In sharp contrast, his involvement in foreign policy was both decidedly personal and highly visible

The pattern was evident from the first days of the new administration, when he explicitly re-centered the foreign policy-making focus within the White House and its National Security Council, headed by Henry Kissinger. He had long resented what he viewed as the elitist culture of the State Department, and especially of its professional Foreign Service—dominated by what he viewed as reflexively liberal career diplomats. His old friend William Rogers would serve as his relatively passive Secretary of State—until Nixon moved in 1973 to incorporate that position into a single command structure by adding the Cabinet office to Kissinger's White House portfolio.

It is worth noting that the Nixon years were part of a pre-cable television age, when national news coverage was largely the province of three major networks. These outlets had inherited a sense of obligatory public service, stemming from a long history of Federal licensing of the public "airwaves." One result was that the networks would normally provide prime-time coverage of a major Presidential address—even though this meant canceling their regular programming and losing the related advertising revenue. It was thus a time when presidents had much easier access than they do now to a powerful "bully pulpit." Nixon made the most of such opportunities to reach a nation-wide audience. His resignation speech opened with the words: "This is the 37th time I have spoken to you from this office…."

Lyndon Johnson had used this format 23 times. Ray Price, in drafting the Resignation Speech left that number blank, suggesting that the press office should provide an exact count. Some critics have argued that Nixon over-used this privilege, but many felt otherwise, given that so many of these speeches were about the ongoing Vietnam War.

Nixon's engagement in the international arena was also dramatized from the outset by his unusual travel schedule. In his first six weeks in office, he visited six European states. In his seventh month in office, he visited seven Asian nations. A year later, he made a nine-day trip that included six European countries. And even as the Watergate pressures closed in tightly on him in 1974 (and undoubtedly because of those intensifying pressures), he spent most of his last month in office abroad, highlighting what he thought of as his greatest remaining strength, his international record, on a three-week trip which included nine countries.

State visits are often regarded as largely ceremonial exercises—reaffirming old alliances, strengthening newer ones. But, from the start, Nixon's itineraries also fit into his longer-range strategies. He surprised the world, for example, with visits during his first summer in office both to Romania to meet with its infamous dictator, Nicolae Ceauşescu, and to Pakistan, to meet with President Yahya Khan. But why? It later became clear that these were among the first steps he took to engage with Communist China, using the relationships that these two hosts had developed with the Peking government as back channels that would lead to Nixon's historic visit there three years later.

If a new China relationship was central to his long-range agenda, it was also a potential step in achieving his most pressing short-term priority, ending the war in Vietnam. The unpopular conflict had ended the career of his predecessor, and Nixon's campaign had centered on his pledge to achieve "peace with honor" in Southeast Asia. Some critics began to talk, sarcastically, about Nixon's "secret plan" to end the war—so little detail did he provide on the campaign trail—but building new relationships with both China and the Soviet Union had been a part of his Vietnam calibrations for some time.

"It's not your war!" This was the advice that Nixon heard from a number of friends and advisors as he entered on his new post, urging him simply to "get out!" It was advice he never considered. For one thing, immediate withdrawal would violate his sense of what it meant to be a strong leader. He would be "bugging out," the first U.S. president to "lose a war." It would also mean betraying many South Vietnamese leaders who had bet their lives on U.S. promises.

An immediate concern grew out of what was widely described as the "Domino Theory," the fear that the fall to Communism of South Vietnam would be quickly followed by Communist takeovers of neighboring countries in Southeast Asia. More than that, a Vietnam setback, Nixon feared, would seriously weaken America's diplomatic credibility all around the world amid the intensifying struggles of the Cold War.

Nixon was also well-positioned to understand, with clarity, what such a defeat could mean on the home political front. As one of the leaders who was asking "who lost China?" in the 1950s, he could now see only too clearly how a frustrated and still formidable Republican right-wing could capitalize on the issue if Vietnam were "lost."

If bugging out was an impossible option from the start, then so, he realized, was the prospect of winning a military victory. The word "quagmire" had already become a familiar way of describing the situation. This was in large measure a guerilla war, after all, often contested by small groups of irregular soldiers, appearing and disappearing amid the jungles and tunnels of the Asian landscape. More than that, the principal motivation of the North Vietnamese was not so much an abstract commitment to the advance of international communism (as many in the West, including

Nixon, often described the matter), but, rather, a long-standing national passion to liberate the whole of Vietnam from the remains of Western colonialism.

If both "bugging out" and "playing to win" were off the table, the remaining possibility for Nixon, was to pursue a "negotiated settlement"—what he would call "peace with honor"—one that would bring American troops home without handing Hanoi a clear victory.

In the end, that was what happened. Sadly, it took much longer (four years) and was far more costly than Nixon had predicted. Some 20,000 U.S. military lives were lost during his first term alone. In the end, of course, Hanoi would win the war. But no dominoes would fall.

While it lasted, the pursuit of an acceptable negotiated settlement was a complex process. Its first requirement was that Hanoi should not expect to achieve military success. The answer was what Nixon called "Vietnamization"—an intense effort to build the South's military capacity and credibility so as to replace US forces over time. The strategy reflected the so-called "Nixon Doctrine," a characteristically centrist approach which called on the U.S. to aid and assist others (abroad and at home) in the pursuit of common objectives, but without trying to do for others what they could (and should) be doing for themselves. The central mystery was just how capably the problematic South Vietnamese government could rise to meet their expanding military challenges. Many have argued that Nixon talked himself into overestimating this potential, having promised to withdraw all US troops before his first term in office ended.

Vietnamization did not mean the hasty withdrawal of US forces, nor did it rule out other strategic military interventions, including the bombing of enemy supply lines and the 1970 incursion of US troops into Cambodia. Nixon himself suggested what some have called the "Madman" tactic, warning Hanoi that that he might lose patience and dramatically widen US attacks on the North.

Henry Kissinger favored more reliance on what he hoped would remain secret American military activities. When news of the U.S. "secret bombing" campaign over Cambodia in 1979 did become public, the

White House reaction was a super-intensive crackdown on press "leaks," one which eventually led to the establishment of the now infamous White House "plumbers" operation.

From the start, however, the key for Nixon was to combine U.S. military action with U.S. military withdrawal under his Vietnamization approach. The combined strategy allowed him to report periodically to the nation on how the number of U.S. personnel in South Vietnam was shrinking from a high of over half a million troops during his opening weeks in office. That messaging, together with the concomitant ending of the military draft, would hopefully dampen the burgeoning rise of domestic war protests. Nixon, with mounting bitterness, came to see domestic protestors as the weak link in his efforts to negotiate an end to the war. Why would Hanoi negotiate if it seemed as though American opinion would eventually force U.S. withdrawal?

As was so often the case with Nixon, all of this meant carefully balancing a series of trade- off considerations. Could the U.S. withdraw quickly enough to cool domestic war resistance, but cautiously enough to give Vietnamization a good chance?

There was yet another component in Nixon's multi-faceted "secret plan:" his hope that the world's two largest Communist powers, China and the Soviet Union, could help encourage the Communist government in Hanoi to seek a negotiated solution. Both provided support for the North Vietnamese military efforts, but neither was as influential a persuader as Nixon might have hoped. Contrary to many western assumptions (including Nixon's), Hanoi's relationship to the international communist cause was less that of a responsive client state and more that of an independent nationalistic liberator.

Nonetheless, engaging with both the USSR and China on the Vietnam front initially seemed to hold important potential. From the start, this centrally involved "playing the China card," understanding that broadening relations with one of the Communist powers would also improve relations with the other. The process became identified as "Triangular Diplomacy," terminology that became closely associated with Henry Kissinger, to the point where some surprised critics assumed that Kissinger must have been the tutor on this matter and Nixon the student. That impression has been strongly contravened over time, as evidence accumulates of Nixon's own early awareness that the USSR and China had a great deal to disagree about, and that the resulting tension was something from which the US could benefit.

He had articulated this view both privately and publicly before his Presidency, including notable expressions in 1967, well before he had even met Kissinger.

He included the Chinese matter at least briefly in a soaring and influential *tour d'horizon* speech in 1967 at the exclusive Bohemian grove encampment of influential business leaders. His message was to demonstrate how China and the USSR were locked in "a bitter struggle for leadership of the Communist world." His address helped appreciably in winning California Republican support for his bid for the GOP presidential nomination—especially when contrasted with Governor Ronald Reagan's charming but much less substantive speech to the same audience.

At the same time, Nixon expanded on the matter in a widely noted article in *Foreign Affairs* magazine, declaring that "we simply cannot afford to leave China forever outside the family of nations, there to nurture its fantasies, cherish its hates and threaten its neighbors. There is no place on this small planet for a billion of its potentially most able people to live in angry isolation." In his formulation, China was still cast in the role of a dangerous old enemy, rather than a potential new friend. "The world cannot be safe until China changes," he warned. Ending China's isolation was one big step on the road to a better world, in his mind. But it also would pave the way for another big step, improving relations with the Soviet Union, a point he notably made in a television appearance on the Tonight Show that same year.

And, in fact, Soviet cooperation on matters such as arms control and trade relations would move ahead impressively in the wake of Nixon's opening to China.

CHAPTER EIGHT

"THE GREAT SILENT MAJORITY"

A useful way to analyze Nixon's evolving Vietnam approaches is to look closely at three television speeches that commanded enormous national attention in his first, second and fourth years in office, analyzing not only the policies they advanced but also the rhetoric that was used in presenting them- and the consequent reactions of the public.

The first of the "Big Three" was the most successful. Delivered on November 3, 1969, it came to be known as the "Silent Majority" speech

As the first anniversary of his election approached, two mounting frustrations faced the President. One was the persistent fervor of the Anti-War movement at home, and the other was the persistent disinterest of the Hanoi government in a negotiated path to peace. And any effort he made to address either one of these challenges risked worsening the other one.

In mid-October a massive set of Washington demonstrations labeled the Moratorium to End the War in Vietnam triggered the Nixon "Silent Majority" speech. A besieged Nixon left the White House for several days to work out his response, alone with his yellow legal pads amid the empty cabins of Camp David, instructing his staff not to interrupt him while he prepared his own text.

His message to the world, supported in considerable detail, was that it was Hanoi that was blocking the path to a negotiated peace, not the

United States. His message to Hanoi was that its path to military victory would always be blocked, as "Vietnamization" took hold. His message to the anti-war protestors was that he respected and shared their long-term goals, if not their short-range priorities. And his message to the American people was that American troops were coming home.

For his conclusion, he found words which harked back to his Orthogonian school days and his sense, even then, that the articulate establishment did not necessarily represent the dominant point of view.

"So tonight, to you, the great silent majority of my fellow Americans, I ask for your support.... For the more divided we are at home, the less likely the enemy is to negotiate at Paris. Because let us understand—North Vietnam cannot defeat or humiliate the United States. Only Americans can do that."

Nixon's approval ratings following the speech soared to 77 percent. A poll of rhetoric scholars ranked it as twenty-first on a list of the most significant American speeches of the twentieth century.

"A Pitiful Helpless Giant?"

Sadly, for Nixon, the second of the "Big Three" speeches undid much of the positive impact that the first speech had achieved. And it set the stage for a newly embattled phase of the Nixon administration, one that would eventually lead to Watergate.

It was delivered just six months after the "Silent Majority" speech, but rather than assuming, as he had in the wake of the November speech, that his strategy had won that silent majority support, April speech seemed to suggest that the support was now disappearing, that he might even become be a one term President, and that a raucous minority had come to dominate the national conversation and ravage the national culture.

The policy initiative that Nixon was describing in the speech was the decision to send U.S. troops into Cambodia —a presumably neutral country that had also served as a sanctuary for North Vietnamese military forces. Their haven was in Parrot's Beak, just 33 miles from the South Vietnamese capital of Saigon. The distance was as close as Baltimore is to Washington, the President emphasized, as he rose from his chair to illustrate the point on an adjacent map. The U.S. goal was to break up the sanctuary and then leave Cambodia. The incursion was supposed to be limited to just forty days—and, in fact, it was. And meanwhile the U.S. was continuing to draw down its overall military presence.

So far, so good. The incursion is portrayed as a vital rear-guard action to help buy time until Vietnamization was complete. Nonetheless, despite the disclaimers, it was easy for many viewers to come away from the speech with the impression that the war was being widened. And that impression was reenforced as the speech proceeded with a shift in Nixon's rhetoric. The goal that he now seems to prioritize is that of avoiding national humiliation—the war rationale seems to be less a matter of geopolitics and more a matter of personal and national psychology—a desire to prove our toughness. The adversary that he most bitterly attacks is the domestic antiwar movement.

"My fellow Americans," he declared, "we live in an age of anarchy, both abroad and at home. We see mindless attacks on all the great institutions which have been created by free civilizations in the last 500 years. Even here in the United States, great universities are being systematically destroyed.... If, when the chips are down, the world's most powerful nation, the United States of America, acts like a pitiful, helpless giant, the forces of totalitarianism and anarchy will threaten free nations and free institutions throughout the world... It is not our power but our will and character that is being tested tonight."

"We will not be humiliated. We will not be defeated," he declares.

The address would be remembered as the "pitiful helpless giant" speech.

In his effort to discredit the protestors in the public eye, he wound up dramatizing their influence. And, in a self-pitying moment (often evident in his private behavior but rarely so clearly highlighted in a public speech), he compares his Cambodia decision to the great wartime decisions made "in this room" by Presidents Wilson, FDR, Eisenhower and Kennedy. And he then acknowledged what he had come to believe was the "fundamental difference" between their successful experiences and his own. "In those decisions, the American people were not assailed by counsels of doubt and defeat from some of the most widely known opinion leaders of the nation."

He reenforces that somewhat self-pitying point by declaring that he would rather be a one term president than becoming the first president to lose a war—and he further reenforces that embattled posture by telling the country that he is not seeking their support for himself but rather for the American troops.

The Thursday evening speech could have been presented as an extension of the strategy described six months earlier, but, as both Hanoi's cold recalcitrance and the protestor's passionate belligerence mounted, Nixon was no longer in a patient mood. Nor was his conservative speechwriter on this occasion, Pat Buchanan. Buchanan reported later that Nixon had ordered him not even to show his draft texts to Henry Kissinger, even after Kissinger asked to see them. (Kissinger later declared that this was the only foreign policy speech Buchanan ever wrote.) Buchanan's rhetoric has been usefully described as the connecting rhetorical link between the Republican party of the 1940s and its super-ardent nationalism and the reappearance of similar attitudes in later—and even the most recent—Republican administrations.

Kissinger described the speech as 'vintage Nixon," but it is unclear whether he saw this as a compliment. It was surely characteristic of the embattled dimension of Nixon's personality—one which was reflected in his repeated viewings of *Patton*, the popular film about the hard-nosed World War II General George Patton, who had been nicknamed "Old Blood and Guts Patton." He reportedly made repeated references to *Patton* in the days leading up to the Cambodia speech.

This writer has suggested earlier in this book that there was more than one "vintage" Nixon—and the contrast between his Vietnam speeches helps to illustrate that point.

Interestingly, when Nixon, 20 years later, was choosing texts to appear in a prospective anthology of his most important speeches (a project in which this writer was briefly involved) the Cambodia incursion speech was the only major address that he did not include, even on his preliminary list.

Nor was the speech a public success. Even within the White House, many staffers wondered uncertainly about how to interpret the apparent change of stakes and strategies. One response was an extensive staff briefing by Henry Kissinger, who helpfully re-emphasized the limited nature of the incursion and its role as a short-term tactic to protect the Vietnamization plan.

Kissinger's calming impact was also evident when he briefed the White House press corps in the ensuing days. Interestingly, after more than a year in office, it was only in the wake of the Cambodia speech that Kissinger became a highly visible public figure. Earlier, his strong German accent, which later was seen as reenforcing his air of authority and expertise, had been seen as a disqualifying reminder of the fictional ex-Nazi scientist Dr. Strangelove.

The audience that responded unhappily to the 'pitiful helpless giant" speech, of course, was the growing anti-war movement. And their anger was further provoked when Nixon, his mood unchanged from the night before, made a symbolic visit the next day to the Pentagon, designed to salute young people in military service. But again, his tone was anything but a calming one:

"You see these bums, you know, blowing up the campuses. Listen, the boys that are on the college campuses today are the luckiest people in the world, going to the greatest universities, and here they are burning up the books, storming around this issue. You name it. Get rid of the war there will be another one."

The word "bums" was quickly quoted around the world.

Protests across the country continued to intensify throughout the weekend, and they exploded when National Guard troops, called in to keep order, fired without apparent provocation into a crowd of demonstrators and non-demonstrators on the campus of Kent State University in Ohio, killing four students and injuring nine others.

Dramatic photographs of the event further triggered a sense of national calamity. The White House press office response seemed to blame the protestors for the tragedy, suggesting that the events "should remind us all once again that when dissent turns to violence it invites tragedy." (In this case, unusually, a draft of the public comment was not shared with the writing staff—and it is not clear that the President approved the exact language. But *The New York Times*, among others, did report it as a direct Presidential quote and it would seem to have reflected Nixon's actual outlook.)

And, of course, his earlier reference to "bums" still lingered in the national consciousness a few days later when the father of Allison Krause, one of the students who had been killed at Kent State, was widely quoted as saying that "my child was not a bum."

Chief of Staff H. R. Haldeman later remembered the period as one that "marked a turning point for Nixon, a beginning of his downhill slide toward Watergate." The President's embattled personal mentality was physically reflected as two rings of busses, parked bumper to bumper, were used to form a protective wall around the White House.

A moment of relief from the administration's "siege mentality" came eight days after the Cambodia speech when Nixon conducted an impressive press conference in the East Room, carefully balanced, neither apologetic nor provocative. Unable to sleep afterward, he spoke by phone with dozens of friends and advisors, then summoned a driver to take him to the Lincoln Memorial where he chatted for a while in the early sunrise hours with crowds of student protestors. It was a potentially important reaching out, but it was marred when early press reports quoted students who emphasized how Nixon, looking for ways to relate, talked about the Syracuse University football team. *The New York Times* described the conversation as "more monologue than dialogue."

Another gesture reaching out in a different direction came a few days later as Nixon's hosted a group of construction workers who had triggered what some called the "Hard Hat Riot" in New York City, angrily assaulting anti-war protestors in what was seen as a symbolic confrontation between an old, blue-collar culture and a new, young," longhair" culture. Nixon was presented and pictured, of course, with a hard hat of his own.

The sense of national and generational polarization deepened as sustained student strikes (eventually involving some four million students) were organized at several hundred colleges and universities, many lasting until the end of the school year. Many of these schools wound up cancelling classes and commencement altogether.

Nixon's Lincoln Memorial visit had meaning for younger members of his own staff, who talked together about ways in which we might help address the sense of alienation that so many of our own generation were then feeling. Initially called together by Hugh Sloan of the communications office, several of us decided that we would individually return to our own home campuses—and perhaps others as well—indicating that we were not coming to persuade or convert, but rather to listen, and that we would report what we heard to the President. Despite all that the rings of busses symbolized, we could at least say we had tried to "communicate."

We all welcomed the opportunity (which, for me, included a visit to Northwestern University, my undergraduate school) to talk with an array of students, administrators, and faculty members. As we returned to Washington to exchange notes, I was asked, as the only speechwriter present, to draft a summary of our thoughts, which we would then share with the President and many of his senior leaders. The President and Attorney General Mitchell were among those who then invited us to sit down and talk about our findings. At heart of our message was our conclusion that most of the antiwar protestors and current student strikers were not intractable enemies nor violence-prone "bums" but rather "the sons and the daughters of the silent majority,"

After a few days had passed, we were surprised to see a *New York Times* story describing this project, including our finding that the student protestors were "the sons and daughters of the silent majority." We were pleased that our message had thus reached a larger audience. I was personally a bit surprised when I learned that some senior administration officials had assumed that I must have been the one who leaked the story—since I had drafted the written report. I made it clear that I was not the leaker of what we had presumed to be a confidential internal message.

And that was the end of the matter—at least for three years. In the summer of 1973, a surprise visitor stopped by my White House office to offer me an apology and a thank you. It was Daniel Patrick Moynihan, about to serve as a U.S. Ambassador, first to India and then to the United Nations, and later (for 24 years) as U.S. Senator from New York.

He explained to me how he had decided, as a very senior Counselor to the President in the difficult spring of 1970, that it would reflect well on the administration to have the public know about our campus visit project and the resulting "sons and daughters" message. He then had quietly leaked the story and our memo to *The New York Times*. When it was rumored that I was the leaker, he wisely decided to preserve his own credibility by remaining silent. And now—three years later—he had come by to fill me in.

CHAPTER NINE

"PEACE WITH HONOR"

Protecting the Withdrawal Strategy

The three major Vietnam speeches under discussion here reflected very different but nonetheless truly "Vintage" Nixons.

The year 1970 continued to be influenced by the embattled rhetoric of April 30, both the frustrations that motivated it and the polarization it engendered. The siege mentality colored not only Nixon's approach to the midterm elections but also that of the U.S. electorate, who bolstered Democratic majorities in the House and the Senate. Nixon would have to work with a Democratic Congress for his entire presidency, sometimes unhappily but often constructively. Rather than buying more time for Vietnamization, the April rhetoric had wound up weakening U.S. public support for the war and, as a result, reducing the incentives for Hanoi to enter meaningful negotiation.

The third of the major Vietnam speeches came two full years later, in May of 1972.

Nixon had re-focused his rhetorical strategy—in his 1971 State of the Union Address for example—away from partisan Republican goals and toward his personal re-election prospects, which did not appear very promising at the time. It would help him enormously if he could deliver on his promises of U.S. troop withdrawals in Vietnam, but it would hurt him fatally if he appeared to have lost the war.

Meanwhile, although troop withdrawals continued, antiwar impatience continued to build. Polls showed that more than 70 percent of Americans felt the War had been a mistake, and 58 percent described it as "immoral." And the opposition had intensified in the summer of 1971 with the publication of the Pentagon Papers, leaked to the press by former Pentagon official Daniel Ellsberg, revealing a pattern over more than two decades of decisions and deceptions that had prolonged the Vietnam conflict.

What was revealed by Ellsberg had happened well before the Nixon years, but the White House reaction to leak of the Pentagon Papers was nonetheless one of outrage, evidently motivated by significant fears of what further embarrassing secrets might later be revealed. Some have speculated that Nixon was afraid that word would get out about his role, just before the 1968 election, in Chennault Affair, which is discussed elsewhere in this volume. What seems more likely is that a general passion for secrecy was an essential part of seeing foreign policy as an intricate "chess game," in which success necessarily required a level of silence that was difficult to achieve in a democratic government.

The "chess" metaphor was later used by Nixon defenders to explain the secrecy of some particularly controversial Cold War interventions. (A prominent non-Vietnam example was US support for the 1973 coup in Chile which unseated the Marxist government and installed the right-wing dictator Augusto Pinochet, who would rule that country for the next seventeen years.)

In any event, the Pentagon Papers controversy touched a sensitive administration nerve. Kissinger publicly described Ellsberg as "the most dangerous man in America." Nixon told staffers to use "any means to "destroy him." The administration also obtained a court order which initially prevented *The New York Times* and *The Washington Post* from publishing more of the secret documents, an order which was reversed by the Supreme Court.

The ferocity of the administration's response against Ellsberg, and against the *Times* and *Post*, not only gave the secret documents enormous increased exposure, but also placed the Nixon administration at the center of the controversy. Nixon's first impulse had been to ignore the matter since it concerned previous administrations, but, again, his latent insecurities also surfaced.

The administration response to the Pentagon Papers disclosure was an intensified anti-leak campaign, including the establishment of a unit that called itself "the Plumbers," whose efforts to discredit Ellsberg would lead to the break in at his psychiatrist's office. Two of the original plumbers later planned the Watergate break-in.

Of course, a great deal of additional planning was also preoccupying Nixon (and Kissinger) in 1971 and early 1972. Nixon's New Economic Policy, announced in August of 1971 (rejecting the traditional link of the US dollar to the "gold standard" while also invoking wage and price controls) was one example, centrally motivated by Nixon's recollection of how recession had cost him the 1960 election.

Importantly, triangular diplomacy was also working well, leading steadily toward a diplomatic opening to China. Kissinger would not only make a secret trip to China, but he was also meeting quite regularly—and secretly—with the Soviet Ambassador, Anatoly Dobrynin. (To keep anyone from noticing, the Ambassador would join the public tourist line at the White House—and a Kissinger aide would then quietly pull him aside after he had entered the building.)

All of this, plus an improved economy in 1972, seemed to brighten the GOP outlook regarding the November elections. Another contributing factor was that much of the Democratic opposition had shifted away from the centrist appeals of the Humphrey campaign team in 1968, finally denying the 1972 nomination to Humphrey's former running mate, Senator Edmund Muskie (who had been beating Nixon in earlier polls)—and delivering it to South Dakota Senator George McGovern, a hero of the more radical left who favored a unilateral U.S. withdrawal from Vietnam.

Nonetheless, Nixon believed that his re-election would be threatened if he did not get U.S. troops entirely (or almost entirely) out of Vietnam by the end of his term, without appearing to have handed Hanoi a victory.

Hanoi clearly understood this Nixon dilemma—as diary entries of the North Vietnamese leaders have more recently revealed. And Nixon understood that they understood his political dilemma, especially as he watched the massive buildup of Northern forces that winter. In response, he had already expanded bombing attacks and was prepared to take further steps when the enemy launched a gigantic Easter Offensive at the end of March in 1972, threatening to capture Saigon itself, or at least to produce an American counter-escalation that could further diminish Nixon's public support at home. The North Vietnamese understood a great deal not only about American politics and elections, but also about Nixon's own temperament.

Nixon quickly grew impatient as the North Vietnamese advances continued that April. He decided it was time to raise the stakes decisively and decided to explain his decision in another major television address on May 8. It was one that he later remembered as one of his proudest moments.

* * *

The military action that Nixon defended in that early May speech was potentially more belligerent and inflammatory than the Cambodia incursion was in 1970. He announced that he was stepping up the bombing of the North, while also mining the harbors of Haiphong, the major North Vietnamese port for receiving arms shipments from the Soviet Union. These moves were again described as a rearguard action, protecting the Vietnamization strategy rather than departing from it. But the rhetorical appeals used in the 1972 speech were very different from the 1970 address—and so was the public reaction.

What Nixon had going for him with the American public at this moment was the fact that most US troops had already been withdrawn, the military draft had ended, the U.S. economy had improved, and his recent China visit was still a fresh and happy memory.

Meanwhile, the Moscow disarmament summit meeting was only two weeks away, and, in that context, even his strong critics were reluctant to mount the anti-Nixon barricades.

Importantly, the military steps were not presented in the speech as a way of showing "how tough we are" but as a cool and calculated way to protect the withdrawal strategy. Nixon also lends credibility to his strategy by slightly moderating the US negotiation stance rather than vehemently attacking the antiwar movement. In fact, he never even mentioned it.

The tone of the address was matter of fact and confident, neither defensive nor self-pitying. It ended with an appeal for direct support not for the troops but for the President. His only other use of direct address was his appeal to people abroad—and particularly in the Soviet Union, expressing his hopes that upcoming Moscow summit would produce the first arms control agreement of the nuclear age.

The great fear, of course, was that the decision to impede Soviet shipping into Haiphong would cause the offended Soviet leader, Leonid Brezhnev, to cancel the summit (as he had recently and explicitly warned he would do). Nixon's escalation decision not only jeopardized his triangular diplomacy strategy, but his re-election prospects as well.

More than that, Henry Kissinger, determined to protect the summit and all that might follow from it, opposed the decision to block Soviet shipping. But Nixon decided to take the risk, fearing that a more passive position, even if it saved the summit, would weaken his bargaining stature in Moscow. It was an enormous, lonely gamble, but it was based on his continuing sense that improving Soviet relations depended on steps that would also serve long-term Soviet interests. Confident that the USSR also wanted the upcoming Moscow summit to succeed, he effectively called Brezhnev's bluff. The Soviet leader backed away from his threat to cancel the meeting, and Nixon won the big stakes poker game.

The decision led not only to the success of the Moscow meetings, but also to later progress on the Vietnam negotiating front, which culminated in a settlement (including the return of U.S. prisoners of war) the following winter. And the entire episode contributed significantly to Nixon's landslide re-election success in November

A personal note: This writer was asked to draft the speech that Nixon would give to the Canadian parliament on the 26th of April—shortly after the Easter offensive had commenced. Nixon was understandably preoccupied with his Vietnam decisions, and he had little time to spend on the Canadian speech. One result was that this writer remembers that Parliament address as the only one of his submitted texts over five years that was delivered by the President with almost no changes.

But there was one problem. In a brief opening paragraph that, obligatorily, referred to the current Vietnam crisis, I slightly altered language that Kissinger had proposed as an appropriate insert. The next thing I knew, I was asked if I could—on very short notice—come to Camp David that night in case the President wanted to revisit the text. After the short helicopter ride and dinner in the staff dining room, I was asked by Alexander Butterfield, the Deputy Chief of Staff, if I would walk with him to Nixon's cabin to see if I could offer any additional assistance. As we stepped into the cabin, we found Nixon sitting alone in the dark, yellow legal pad in hand, fireplace aglow, contemplating the wooden scene outside his cabin window. And he was also, most probably, pondering the lonely war -escalation decision he was about to make.

Nixon leapt to his feet as we entered the cabin, and immediately turned his attention to welcoming me—warmly but nervously: "Did you have a good dinner? Did you have time for dessert? Would you like to watch a movie? Or go bowling? or skeet shooting? —wait, no it's too dark out for that!" The considerate welcome, I later learned, may have been partly in compensation for his earlier reaction back in Washington over the wording of that introductory paragraph.

The choice of words for the opening of the speech turned out to be easily adjusted, and Nixon's concern undoubtedly reflected the unusual decision-making pressures of the moment. At any rate, it resulted in his instruction (later ignored) that an expert foreign policy speechwriter should be appointed to Kissinger's staff—rather than involving the regular Writing and Research staff. On my visit to the Presidential archives a few years later, the archivist looked up my name to demonstrate how the library system worked, and the first item to pop out onto the computer screen was a note from Haldeman's diary regarding the President's review of my Canada draft : "Typical Nixon tantrum."

We went on to Canada the next day, and the speech went well. The line that provoked the warmest reaction was one that Nixon improvised after observing the protocol of delivering his opening greeting in French: "I trust you will give me allowances for trying to speak in the language that I studied 37 years ago. When I tried it out, the day before I came, on the top linguist in the American Government, General Walters, he said, 'Go ahead. You speak French with a Canadian accent.'"

And so the critical year proceeded, a mix of challenges and successes. And it ended not only with a landslide win, but with Nixon's three great foreign policy goals in hand, the China and Soviet breakthroughs and (almost) peace in Vietnam.

But Nixon's reactions were less than ecstatic. "A strange melancholy came over me," he later recalled. The election was "one of the most frustrating and in many ways the least satisfying of all." In a somewhat typical moment of Nixonian frustration he abruptly greeted his staff at the White House the next day, not with words of appropriate celebration, but by asking them all to submit letters of resignation (most of which would not be accepted.) He then retreated into the silence of Camp David, ordered the extended Christmas Day "carpet bombing" of Hanoi, and began to plan for a radical reorganization of the executive branch, one that would make cabinet departments more directly responsive to the White House itself.

One factor in his disappointed and self-isolating reactions may have been that for the third biennial election in a row, his party had failed to carry either the House or the Senate. His campaign had been a highly personal effort, offering relatively little White House support to state and local candidates. *The Washington Post's* political guru, David Broder, described it as an "extremely lonely victory."

Also, as the second term opened, another major factor lurked just below the surface of events.

And so, to Watergate.

CHAPTER TEN

A THIRD-RATE BURGLARY —AND ITS AFTERMATH

If an impulse to oversimplify has characterized public memories of Richard Nixon's career, this tendency has been especially evident with respect to his terminal Watergate crisis.

Convenient myths have dominated the Watergate writings not only of Nixon's most strident attackers but also of his strongest defenders.

Many of his defenders, in this writer's view, have complicated Nixon's ongoing image by insisting that Watergate was essentially a Democratic super-plot to unseat him, perhaps even a scheme designed "to make Ted Kennedy President." This alleged plotting has been described by some as "lawfare"—essentially the waging of war by legal means, involving "vast conspiracies," "secret cabals," "illicit rendezvous," and repeated violations of due process. Former Nixon aide, Geoff Shepard, has championed these theories in a series of books; they became the basis for a film and even, in 2024, the brief run of an off-Broadway play in which Nixon was given the final trial that his resignation had avoided 50 years earlier. At the ending of that play, with the theater audience acting as the jury, only once over 29 performances was Nixon found guilty.

The Shepard approach not only dramatized the perfidy of Nixon's opponents, but it also tried to rationalize away key pieces of anti-Nixon evidence. Among them, for example, were excerpts from the Nixon tapes which Shepard himself, from his White House office, had originally described as the "smoking gun" that would cement the legal case against the President. One such recording captured Nixon's request that the FBI defer to the CIA in investigating the Watergate break-in. The fact that neither the CIA nor the FBI went along with the request was seen by Shepard and others as demonstrating Nixon's legal innocence. Similarly, when Nixon seemed to approve the payment of hush money to one of the burglars, the actual payment of that hush money was said to have happened slightly later and thus could not, presumably, be directly linked to Nixon's instruction.

Thus, even the "smoking gun tapes," which had demonstrated Nixon's culpability in the eyes of so many observers, absolved him in the eyes of some defenders because they fell short of proving legal criminality.

Nixon himself later tried to muffle the impact of the damaging tapes by pointing to what they did *not* say: he had never proposed clemency for the Watergate burglars, which he could have done, he said, "and the whole thing would have gone away." Whether that is true or not, what the public came to wonder with growing impatience as the weeks and months went by is whether a complete and forceful investigation of the entire scandal, led by the President himself, might have made the "the whole thing go away" more quickly and convincingly. It was not just what Nixon may have done that bothered the public, but also the things he might have done—and did not do.

Neither technical assertions of Nixon's legal innocence nor arguments about illegal plotting on the part of his enemies have been ultimately effective in shifting Watergate blame away from Nixon. What the public at the time (and even since) could not forgive in the Watergate case was being lied to about it. The impact of what Nixon said at the time—and of what he did not say—created a crisis of public confidence, as he later recognized. One can even imagine that, at the time, a confession of total involvement would have been a better choice for the President, bringing an early sense of cloture and at least curtailing what Gerald Ford in his first sentence as the new President would describe as "our long national nightmare."

But it is also worth noting that, despite the nightmare which drove him from office, Nixon himself was able to reclaim a measure of credibility with his own, later Watergate reflections. In his extensive series of television interviews with David Frost in 1977, for example, he shared his candid views.

"I let down my friends, I let down the country. I let down our system of government and the dreams of all those young people that ought to get into government but will think it is all too corrupt and the rest. ...I let the American people down, and I have to carry that burden with me for the rest of my life. ..."

Nor did he even hint at the excuse that a plot by his opponents is what ended his Presidency. What brought him down? "I brought myself down... I gave them a sword—and they stuck it in, and they twisted it with relish. And I guess if I'd been in their position, I'd have done the same thing."

"I didn't stop it," he acknowledged about the coverup. "It was so botched up. I made so many bad judgments. The worst ones, mistakes of the heart rather than the head... But let me say a man in that top job, he's got to have a heart, but his head must always rule his heart."

Nixon's confessions, it can be argued, have served his memory much better over the long run than the over- simplifications of his defenders.

At the same time, oversimplifications have also abounded in the work of Nixon's critics, sometimes using the Watergate affair to amplify their picture of Nixon as an unmitigated villain. His motive in covering up Watergate, some critics now argue, was to to cover up a series of earlier crimes. In his recent book called *Watergate, A New History* (2023), Garrett Graff describes the broad White House culture under Nixon as conspiratorial and corrupt, so that Watergate is seen as the inevitable outcome of a drama that began even before Nixon's election. In this context, a wide variety of presidential actions are recast as essentially malevolent (including, for example, Nixon's handling of the Pentagon Papers challenge.) Indeed, in Graff's view, the central motivation for covering up from 1972 to 1974 turns out to be Nixon's fear of being blamed for the delay in Vietnam peace talks just before his first election in 1968, the so-called Chennault Affair.

Madam Anna Chennault was a leading figure in the exiled Overseas Chinese community after the Chinese Communist Revolution, a leading Republican fundraiser and an active Nixon supporter. She had long been in close touch with the South Vietnamese government and its President, Nguyễn Văn Thiệu.

As the 1968 campaign entered its final days, Nixon learned that President Johnson was about to propose an immediate resumption of the suspended Vietnam peace negotiations, a step that was likely to turn the very close election race in Humphrey's favor.

In the end, the impact of Johnson's decision was much diluted when the South Vietnamese announced that they would not participate in the new negotiations. But a remaining question in many minds was whether Nixon himself had worked to encourage the Saigon refusal. Had he, for example, directed Madam Chennault to persuade the Saigon government that they would get a better deal by waiting for a new Nixon administration to negotiate a more helpful settlement?

The comprehensive Nixon biography by John Farrell (*Nixon: The Life*, 2017)) has more recently revealed that Nixon did explicitly ask his aide, H.R. Haldeman, to find a way to "monkey wrench" the approaching Johnson initiative, an effort that could be seen as treasonous interference by a private citizen in a critical foreign policy initiative. At the time, Johnson himself reportedly used the "word "treason" with respect to the alleged Nixon effort, though he never said that publicly.

In the end, most observers have concluded that Nixon can be absolved of the charge that he helped to delay the settlement and thus risked extending the war. For one thing, the Saigon government would not have needed Chennault's prodding to veto the peace talk renewal, nor would Chennault and company have needed Nixon's urging to prod the South Vietnamese. Indeed, there was never any direct evidence that the Nixon camp had approached Chennault about the matter, nor that Chennault prodded Saigon. In the end, the peace talks were resumed in the new year, but again, without any progress.

Interest in the so-called "Chennault Affair" originally centered on whether Nixon's (or Chennault's) behavior had in some way jeopardized the renewal of peace talks and thus helped to extend the Vietnam War. That now seems to have been unlikely. But the continuing significance of the Chennault affair now seems to lie in the suggestion that Nixon's fears about the matter becoming public knowledge could help explain his Watergate coverup. This suspicion explains the announcement early in 2026 that the new museum at the Watergate building would now add to its portrait exhibition of Watergate-related figures a painting of Mme. Chennault.

* * *

What else can one say here about the Watergate period from the perspective of a former Nixon staff member? One impression is that no one at the White House at the time really knew very much at all about what was really was going on, and that this was probably also true for the President himself. It was clear that "the crazies" (led by Gordon Liddy) had arranged for and then bungled the break-in of the Democratic headquarters, and that other, similarly reckless efforts to "gather intelligence" about the other side, or to disrupt their campaign events, had gotten far out of hand. But just who else might have been implicated in the planning or the financing of all of this remained a lurking mystery.

A result of the confusion, and Nixon's failure to resolve it, was that the rumors worsened, the doubts increased, and the public grew increasingly weary. The" third-rate burglary" (as White House Press Secretary Ron Ziegler originally termed it) continued to occupy more and more emotional space in the public mind. The term "Watergate" soon became the convenient catch-all label for a broad host of Nixon administration abuses, just as the "-gate" suffix later became attached to a wide variety of unrelated public scandals.

It is often forgotten that more than two years of uncertainty passed between the Watergate break-in June of 1972 and Nixon's resignation in August of 1974. It is also surprising in retrospect to realize how little impact Watergate initially had on Nixon's public standing. He won the November 1972 election (five months after the Watergate break-in) by the largest margin in US history (61 percent to 39 percent). He sailed into a second term with a Vietnam war settlement in place—marked by the consequent opportunity to welcome returning US prisoners of war at a stirring White House celebration.

But the tide would quickly turn. Some nine months after the break-in itself, in March of 1973, James McCord, one of the burglars, would tie the plot quite directly to the Committee to Re-Elect the President (CREEP—as it conveniently became known.) The ensuing wave of investigations, by the Congress, the press and Nixon's own Justice Department would culminate in the President's resignation some 17 months later.

Most visible were dramatic public hearings before the newly created Senate Select Committee on Presidential Campaign Activities, headed by Senator Sam Ervin, for several months in 1973. Nixon might well have survived the furor if it had not been for the Committee's discovery that summer that many of his office conversations had been tape-recorded, a fact that was publicly confirmed that July by former White House Deputy Chief of Staff Alexander Butterfield.

Suddenly there seemed to be a way to answer the question that had been repeated so often at the Committee's earlier hearings: "What did the President know, and when did he know it?" Not surprisingly, the tapes were immediately subpoenaed, not only by the Committee but also by the recently appointed special Watergate Prosecutor, Archibald Cox. Nixon's refused to release them, citing the concept of "executive privilege," a claim that a skeptical pubic widely interpreted as a sign that they might contain damaging information.

* * *

"I am not a crook!"

The Watergate story for that last year of the Nixon Presidency was focused on the battle for the tapes, with the issue finally being resolved when the Supreme Court decided unanimously in the summer of 1974 to order the release of the "smoking gun" tape that led directly to Nixon's resignation.

Throughout that last year, tapes-related questions had dominated the news. One early controversy focused on an 18 and a half minute gap on the tape of Nixon's office conversation immediately after the Watergate break-in. Had Nixon himself erased that portion of the recording? Observers recalled Nixon's life-long awkwardness with small physical tasks, which was one of the reasons he had set up a voice-activated taping system in the first place, rather than one that he could turn on and off manually as Lyndon Johnson had done. As was noted earlier in this account, Nixon's biographer, Jonathan Aitken, had opened his book by noticing how much difficulty Nixon had in handling the sugar tongs during one of their meals together.

What seemed less plausible was the White House claim that Nixon's senior assistant, Rose Mary Woods, had accidentally erased that material by leaving her foot on the wrong pedal while she stretched across the office to answer the telephone. Again, this clumsy coverup story backfired. The restaged photos of the implausible "Rose Mary stretch" were greeted with widespread skepticism.

The most dramatic of the tapes-related controversies, and the most damaging for Nixon, was one that he brought on himself. Dubbed "The Saturday Night Massacre," it took place on October 20, 1973, when Nixon ordered Attorney General Elliott Richardson to fire Archibald Cox, only to have Richardson, as well as his deputy, William Ruckelshaus, refuse and resign in protest.

The public reaction was one of considerable alarm—the legal system itself seemed under threat. Some commentators described the developments as an attempted *"coup d'*état," invoking third world comparisons. Public nerves were only slightly calmed when Nixon, a few days later, agreed to appoint a new Special Prosecutor, Leon Jaworski, under whom the Watergate investigations would continue.

The news reporting on that Saturday night in October had a decidedly alarmist tone. "The country tonight is in the midst of what may be the most serious constitutional crisis in its history," was how anchorman John Chancellor of NBC News summed things up. My own over-reaction was to leap up from a pleasant dinner party and dash to the White House to "rescue" my private papers from whatever might have been coming. Similarly, another guest at the same dinner rushed off to join colleagues at the Special Prosecutor's office, which had now been seized and shut down by the FBI—as had the offices of the Attorney General. Chancellor also described that situation in memorable terms: "That's a stunning development and nothing even remotely like it has happened in all of our history."

The intense Watergate fixations of 1973 took on a different character after the Saturday Night Massacre. Within hours, an impeachment resolution was introduced in the House of Representatives, notably by a Republican member, Margaret Heckler of Massachusetts. It was one of 21 such new resolutions. Impeachment hearings began almost immediately.

I had known Richardson in earlier years when he was Lieutenant Governor of Massachusetts and an early supporter of the progressive Republican research group, the Ripon Society, which I had headed for a while. I almost took a writing job with him in 1973 and would then have presumably exited with him at the time of the Saturday Night Massacre. Instead, my immediate response to the Massacre was to accept a position in New York, although I stayed on long enough at the White House to again help prepare the longer, written version of Nixon's annual State of the Union message (discussed elsewhere in this account), leaving in early February of 1974, six months before Nixon left.

Although the Massacre persuaded many observers that the tapes must have contained damning evidence, Nixon had nonetheless also accomplished his immediate goal. Archibald Cox—with his strong Kennedy connections—was now gone. Amid the furor, the White House decided to back off for the moment, and, as a new Special Prosecutor took up his mantle, the public clamor briefly subsided.

But the investigations did not. And, as the weeks went by, the range of so-called Watergate concerns also broadened. A variety of apparently unrelated matters suddenly were seen as relevant. On example was the so-called Huston plan (proposed, but never activated, much earlier by a White House aide who once headed an embattled conservative organization called Young Americans for Freedom). The Plan's aim was to wage a more intensive war against presumed far-left conspirators, partly by intercepting their mail. Another new concern included a host of campaign "dirty tricks", presumably supervised by a friendly associate named Donald Segretti, which were compared by some Nixonites to the work of the "trickster" Dick Tuck, whose mischief had plagued some of Nixon's earlier campaigns. The "tricks"—on all sides—were most often a matter of rude signage and other disrupting tactics at opponents' campaign rallies.

Other developments reenforced public impressions of runaway White House misbehavior: not only the gap on the tapes, but also the reported existence of Nixon's so-called "enemies list" and its alleged misuse by tax investigators. In the middle of the tumult came the story of how Vice President Spiro Agnew had received cash bribes at his White House offices relating to favors he had performed during his Maryland Governor years. Agnew's October resignation was widely seen as enhancing the possibility that Nixon would eventually be forced out of office, since Agnew's successor, former Michigan Congressman Gerald Ford, was seen as a more plausible successor to the Presidency than Agnew might have been.

And, of course, fundamental questions about the President's own trustworthiness persisted: why couldn't Nixon have done more to control the "crazies," to temper the increasingly embattled "us versus them" White House culture, and to address directly the growing epidemic of public mistrust.

The White House and its defenders tried to handle the matter in a variety of ways. Central to their response was the continuing absence of direct evidence that Nixon himself had ordered the break in, or had even known about it or about many of the other so-called Watergate abuses. Accompanying these arguments from Nixon defenders were steady reminders (often counterproductive ones) that the complaints should be seen as "routine political hardball," that "everyone does it," that the offenses themselves were only "small potatoes," the work of "a few clowns." Even before the release of the smoking gun tapes pointed to more direct Nixon involvements, public mistrust intensified.

Nixon inadvertently handed his adversaries a useful tool during a late 1973 press conference at Florida's Walt Disney World. He was responding to growing concerns about his presumed financial misbehavior—low tax payments and questionable deductions. He forcefully repudiated such charges, concluding decisively with the words: "People have got to know whether or not their President is a crook. Well, I am not a crook!"

It says a lot about the transformed mood of the moment that the financial context of his words was quickly forgotten, and his summary phrase, "I am not a crook," came to live on as a symbol of his Watergate coverup sins. I routinely ask students in my course about Nixon to write down the first words that come to their minds when they think of Nixon. More than 50 years since his resignation, the phrase "I am not a crook" has consistently dominated these student recollections.

Perhaps Nixon's most elaborate effort to deal with the tapes controversy was to release a written transcript of critical tape recordings in April of 1974. But this effort also backfired. The transcripts quickly became objects of public ridicule because they were so frequently dominated by the parenthetic phrase "expletive deleted." The phrase recurred dozens upon dozens of times, leading some to the vivid impression that that the private Nixon was a particularly profane conversationalist. In fact, later reviews showed that an overwhelming percentage of the deleted expletives were milder words like "hell or "damn" or "son-of-a bitch"—but that was not the impression that the public took away.

The "expletive deleted" issue became a key contributor to the badly tarnished Nixon portrait that was eventually revealed by the tapes. As more of the tapes were transcribed and publicized, the President's "dark side" came into clearer public view. His resentments and prejudices, his casual use of antisemitic language, his demeaning references to intellectuals, all commanded increasing attention, even apart from the specific 'smoking gun' passages that tied him to the coverup and forced his resignation. Of the 3000 plus hours of taped conversations, only about 200 hours related to Watergate, but they have had a lasting impact on the way the public has come to think about the Nixon personality. (Or personalities?)

His defenders have usefully pointed out that a good part of the offensive language he often used (both casually and especially during fits of temper) may have emerged from his desire, over the years, to be seen as "one of the boys." In practice, his defenders point out, he behaved in distinctly different ways, relying, for example, on a number of close Jewish and Ivy League advisors, Nonetheless, the Nixon that the world discovered through the tapes must be seen as another "vintage Nixon."

I had left the White House staff early in the winter of 1974, but Watergate-related questions continued to be a haunting preoccupation, and one from which only Nixon's resignation finally provided relief. White House press spokesman Gerry Warren had announced my departure by saying that I was leaving "with the best of feelings toward the White House." But that truth was complicated by the fact that I also left with a lot of questions. Should I share any of this publicly?

An opportunity to discuss the matter at a New York City church service provided one immediate outlet for expressing my feelings (an invitation to speak at a national church conference would have provided another—except that the organization cancelled it, reluctant to provide a platform for what they wrongly assumed would be pro-Nixon propaganda.) After much hesitation, I finally agreed to an interview with the veteran New York Times reporter R. W. Apple. Under the headline "Ex-Nixon Writer Talks of Scandal," his account emphasized how "still reluctant" I was, just weeks after resigning, "to deliver any general judgments about Watergate," quoting me as being "bewildered and surprised and skeptical and shocked and above all sad."

That same feeling persisted among many former Nixon aides, until his resignation provided the sense of cloture and relief that we felt both we—and he—needed. A few of us shared a common reaction the morning after Nixon's televised retirement speech in August: "It seems as though the sun has come out again!"

As the leaks, rumors, and surprises intensified that spring, it had become routine for some of us on the White House staff to join many other Watergate-addicts at the corner of 15th and L Streets, where the next day's *Washington Post* would first appear for sale (near the newspaper's headquarters). In this way we could get a first look at what new Watergate details might there be revealed. Watergate preoccupations were inescapable it seemed, even at the Shoreham Hotel's Blue Room, where night after night, the comedian Mark Russell would ruminate on Watergate matters, with the repeated reminder: "I am not making this stuff up folks; it's just rip and read, right off the ticker!"

It was during that Watergate-obsessed Spring that I met Carl Bernstein at a friend's home. He was, of course, the junior journalist at *The Washington Post* who was initially assigned on that June weekend to cover what seemed like a minor, local crime story: and who, with his colleague Bob Woodward, played a major role in keeping the story alive during the following year. Their journalistic advantage was that as junior reporters, without a pre-existing range of high-level connections, they were ready to search for leads among lots of "little people." All I could share when Bernstein later phoned me were my observations about the mood of the White House staff. But I was able to learn more about where the Watergate matter was heading from the questions he asked. An example: "Did you ever hear about a White House voice-taping system?" (This was well before the tapes existence was confirmed at the Ervin Committee's summer hearings.)

In normal times, journalists would compare notes about who had the best sources at the White House or in other government circles. But at this point in the Watergate drama the situation was reversed—we would rush to share notes with other White House staff members about our sources at the Washington Post or other press outlets. My colleague David Gergen, for example, would relay similar leads from his acquaintance, Bob Woodward. It became even clearer to us that the place where Watergate was "happening" during that scandal-obsessed year was not at the White House but in the newsrooms of the journalism world.

Years later, a less-consequential question came to dominate post-Watergate speculations, i.e. the identity of "Deep Throat." Who was this secret source made famous in Woodward and Bernstein's book *All the President's Men* and the Oscar-winning 1976 film with the same title. (The book and film had something of an adulatory impact on the journalism profession, even spurring a surge in journalism school applications.)

Nixon's senior aide Len Garment discussed the Deep Throat question in dramatic language in the year 2000 with his book *"In Search of Deep Throat: The Greatest Political Mystery of Our Time."* The book provided a thoughtful reflection on the conflicting ethical claims of loyalty to one's patrons versus the public responsibility of a potential whistle-blower. It also speculated a bit wildly about the precise identity of the mysterious source. (Among his potential suspects was Pat Buchanan.)

In 2005, after 30 years of fruitless public speculation, Deep Throat revealed himself; he was W. Mark Felt, the former Associate Director of the FBI, a claim that Woodward and Bernstein quickly confirmed. Until that moment, they believed that only their editor Ben Bradlee had known his identity. The story prompted thoughtful discussions that still continue in journalistic circles about the use and misuse by reporters of unnamed confidential sources, who should approve their use and know their identity, and how such sources (and their motivations) should be publicly characterized.

"But My President Didn't Do That"

It was primarily journalists who kept the Watergate story alive from June of 1972 until the spring of 1973. A bit later, the momentum would move to another stage, the Senate Watergate hearings, which became a national fixation as witnesses like Nixon's chief White House Counsel, John Dean, shared revealing stories about Nixon's private reactions to the Watergate affair, including his own warning to Nixon that there was "a cancer on the Presidency." Ben Bradlee described the obsession with the Ervin Committee hearings: "You could walk down the street, and every store, every office, every bar had the hearings on.... You couldn't get away from it!" (My family tried to get away from it all briefly with a relaxing vacation in the English countryside, including an initial stop at a place called —believe it or not: "John Dean's Bar and Grill.")

In Nixon's eyes, of course, the coverup was justified because it protected his continuing pursuit of "a generation of peace." He also later explained that he was motivated by loyalty to his administration friends, whom he regarded in a sense as his clients, for whom he could help play the role of defense attorney. His defenders have emphasized that many of the rumored plots never went very far, including the Huston plan, the IRS Enemies list, and the Nixon suggestion that Watergate should be handled by the CIA. In their view, the hysteria over Watergate was vastly exaggerated.

But leading members of the Congress increasingly disagreed, including a substantial bi-partisan majority of House Judiciary Committee members, led by Democratic Congresswoman Barbara Jordan of Texas who put the matter forcibly when she declared: "I am not going to sit here and be an idle spectator to the diminution, the subversion, the destruction of the Constitution."

Another key committee voice was that of Lawrence Hogan of Maryland (whose son later became Governor of that state). He was the first Republican member to call for Nixon's impeachment, summing up powerfully what became a strong Congressional consensus:

> "The thing that is so appalling to me, is that the President, when this whole idea was suggested to him, didn't in righteous indignation rise up and say 'Get out of here. You are in the office of the President of the United States. How can you talk

> about blackmail and bribery and keeping witnesses silent? This is the Presidency of the United States!' But my President didn't do that. He sat there, and he worked and worked to try to cover this thing up so it wouldn't come to light."

The Committee voted 28 to 10 on one resolution, for impeachment, and even the ten who voted for Nixon in committee later said that they changed their minds after the taped evidence became available. Would the full House endorse that verdict—and, if so, would the Senate then find the President guilty? A small Congressional delegation, including the recent GOP Presidential nominee, Barry Goldwater, told Nixon that the Senate, with Goldwater's support, would do just that.

Tom Wicker, the longtime political columnist of *The New York Times* and a frequent Nixon critic, later published a book about Nixon with the controversial title *One of Us: Richard Nixon and the American Dream* (1991). Wicker portrays Nixon, with his life-long "outsider spirit," as mirroring both the strengths and weaknesses of the American psyche, including, when it counted the most, an ultimate respect for democratic processes. Wicker's final sentence underscores a preeminent point: "But surely Nixon was one of us, too, at our occasional best, when in the blackest hours of his life he managed to rise above his bitterness and his cynicism, refusing to challenge the legitimacy of Kennedy's election and peacefully surrendering the tapes that ruined him, when the Supreme Court commanded."

The tapes that were released on August 5th included the so-called "smoking gun" tape—linking Nixon more directly to the coverup. Over the long run, the tapes may have dealt Nixon the most devastating blow, not only by revealing more details about the Watergate coverup, but by revealing a lot more about the dark side of Nixon's complex personality.

As the suspense built, chief White House speechwriter Ray Price, prepared two drafts of a national address for Nixon, one resigning and one holding out. Both began with a phrase that emphasized their historical importance: "This is the 37th time I have spoken to you from this office where so many decisions have been made that shaped the history of this nation." The impressive number did not appear in Price's draft—that space was left blank, and the press office was asked at the last moment to recall the exact number.

Nixon delivered the resignation speech on the evening of August 8. He signed his formal one-sentence resignation letter the next morning. He later recalled how he had awakened in the middle of "my last night in the White House," unable to escape the chants of "Jail to the Chief" from the still hovering street crowds, and discovering that, coincidentally, the battery on his watch had run out.

He awakened to a sympathetic farewell moment with members of his residency staff and then proceeded to say goodbye his presidential staff in the East Room, on his way to the White House helicopter pad and his flight into retirement. That final farewell speech was shared nationally through live network news coverage (to Pat Nixon's dismay as she felt this intimate gathering should not be on public display). But fortunately, it was, both for the country and for Nixon's later reputation.

These final remarks have been remembered as typical of Nixon, particularly as he reflected on his own "outsider" history. He went on, as we have seen earlier in this account, to recall his mother, Hannah, as "a saint" and to remember his father. But the speech was also deeply Nixonian in another important way, the final, telling moment of self-appraisal with which he summed up much of his life—and his presidency:

"Always remember: others may hate you, but those who hate you don't win unless you hate them. And then you destroy yourself."

CHAPTER ELEVEN

THE FINAL TWO DECADES

Nixon's first post-resignation challenge was a severe health crisis in the form of phlebitis, an inflammation of the veins that required surgery to prevent the blood clot from migrating from his leg to the brain. The illness led to speculation by some that it may have influenced Ford's decision to pardon him, though a much more likely explanation was Ford's genuine desire to move the country out of the Watergate nightmare and into a refreshed future. Nonetheless, the controversial pardon was widely thought to have been a factor in Ford's reelection defeat by Jimmy Carter in 1976. (The Kennedy family echoed what was then a widespread bipartisan sentiment concerning the pardon when, 25 years later, they presented Ford with their "Profile in Courage" award.)

Nixon recovered well from his post-resignation health crisis and went on to live for another 20 years, re-establishing over time his image as a senior statesman. He settled in San Clemente, California, earlier the site of his western White House, and then moved back again in 1980 to the "action" in the New York area, living there until his death in April of 1994. Pat Nixon had passed away a year earlier.

The former president published nine new books in these years, including his detailed Memoirs and another autobiographical reflection called *In the Arena.* He wrote several books about foreign affairs that helped restore something of his public image as a senior statesman. He was widely consulted by a wide of influential leaders. William Safire, his former speechwriter who had become a Pulitzer-winning *New York Times* columnist, remembered such sessions not only for Nixon's insights into the issues of the moment but also his precise calibration of the time available for conversation, and his insistence that a few minutes be reserved for discussing the current sports scene.

I saw Nixon from time to time during these years, including one memorable encounter in the maternity ward at the New York hospital where his grandson, Christopher Cox, had just been born. My wife and I were among ten couples who ran into Nixons in the corridor outside the delivery rooms as we were briefed on what to do when our own babies arrived in the next few days. After I had alerted an accompanying Secret Service officer to my Nixon ties, the former President stopped to greet us. Uncomfortable, as always, with casual small talk, he began by asking the ten very pregnant women, "and just what is it that all of you are doing here? "And then, recovering quickly, he continued. "Oh of course. Some of you are going to have little girls and some of you are going to have little boys." Then, with a smile: "And those who have little girls, you can sing that song from the film *Gigi* that I love so well, "Thank Heaven for Little Girls.'" As he turned to leave, he suddenly remembered the little boy vote. He hesitated and turned back to the group. "And what about those are will have little boys?" Slamming his fist into his hand, he ended the visit by declaring: "Well. I guess you'll just have to go out and by him a football helmet!" And he spun quickly away to join Pat in a nearby elevator.

* * *

Even at the lowest ebb of his standing with the American public, Nixon retained a highly favorable image in other parts of the world. Not surprisingly, this was true in China. But it also was true in places like France. On a visit to Paris shortly after leaving the White House, I was surprised to find that the French continued to hold Nixon in high regard. They attributed his Watergate problems to American naïvéte, not to Nixon's misbehavior. As one man put it, "The French would not want a President who did not wiretap his opponents." New French acquaintances were inevitably surprised when the found out that, while I had recently been working for Nixon, I also shared some of his critics' questions.

More than a decade later, I had opportunity to share in a special Nixon moment in Paris, when he was honored in 1987 by the Académie des Beaux-Arts. He had been invited to become a Foreign Associate of the Academy, replacing the recently deceased master pianist Artur Rubinstein. In the French tradition, he had been invited to speak about Rubinstein. He ended his address recalling his attendance early in his presidency, at Charles de Gaulle's memorial service at Notre Dame cathedral. He remembered how deeply moved he was as that service ended and the church organ suddenly "spoke to the hearts of the French people" by sounding the forceful notes of *La Marseillaise*, the French national anthem.

"Such is the power of music," he concluded. "Such was the gift of Maestro Rubinstein."

And What If He Had Stayed?

The recent readiness to reconsider Nixon's public life—and to give more attention to a wider range of his accomplishments—has included a new readiness to ask what would have happened if he had stayed in office. While the hypothetical suggestions are complex and controversial, some are worth noting.

The speculation, of course, includes the fact that the Nixon who stayed on would have been a very different Nixon in the public's eye in his second term than in his first four years. Among other things, while his image when he first took office was that of a "two-time loser" who squeaked into office with just 43 percent of the popular vote, he opened his second term as a two-time winner, reelected with 61 percent of the vote.

The public sense that Nixon's first term had been a relative success fortified his confidence that his second term could be a triumphant one. He thought a great deal about what could happen and appears to have concluded that even if Congress would not cooperate fully, he could accomplish a great deal by executive action.

Of course, there is also a distinct possibility that Nixon might have given vent to some of his uglier impulses in his second term, as he threatened to do in tape-recorded conversations from the fall of 1972. Referring to earlier threats to use the Justice Department and the FBI against his "enemies list," he fulminated:, "they are asking for it and they are going to get it.... We have not used the power in this first four years...we have not used the Bureau, and we have not used Justice. But things are going to change now. And they are either going to do it right or go."

It was a typical Nixon rant—one that has been echoed, and even acted upon, at the Presidential level in more recent years. But, like so many of Nixon's rants, it went nowhere. And it seems even less likely to have been acted upon if Nixon had been a successful second term President.

High on the re-elected President's priorities list in 1973 was a series of organizational reforms of the executive branch, growing out of the extensive studies during his first term of the President's Advisory Council on Executive Organization, headed by Roy Ash, the president of Litton Industries. The Ash Council had already proposed the successful creation of the Office of Management and Budget (OMB) and the Environmental Protection Agency (EPA). But it had outlined even more ambitious steps to make the sprawling executive branch work more effectively, reducing the number of cabinet departments, for example, and strengthening the ability of the President to control the long-feared bureaucracy. Without Watergate, Nixon would surely have moved forward with this project—and may well have succeeded.

Other reforms that had been stalled in the Congress during the first term were also likely candidates for revival, including far-reaching domestic innovations such as national health insurance and national welfare systems (including a guaranteed minimum income provision). And again, the sheer margin of his re-election victory persuaded many that Congress would now assume a more supportive posture, or that progress on these and other fronts could be made without Congressional action.

If Nixon had completed two full terms in office it seems likely that his practical, moderating influence on Republican politics would also have been enhanced. He would not have prevented—nor perhaps even tried to prevent—the Reagan takeover that had begun in earnest in 1976, when Reagan launched a primary challenge to Gerald Ford. But his 1972 election triumph also found him promoting a new future for the GOP, in which his own leadership role might have tempered what eventually became the complete disappearance of progressive leadership within the party's ranks.

The international scene might also have evolved in different ways had Watergate never happened. In post-retirement interviews, for example, Nixon emphasized his close relationship with the Shah of Iran. He speculated that, as a respected former President, he might have helped strengthen not only the American government's commitment to the Shah, but also its opposition the extreme authoritarian nature of Ayatollah Khomeini, the leader of the radical Iranian revolution. The troubled and turbulent history of Iran and the Middle East might have been different, many have said, if the embattled Shah had received stronger Western support and been able to progress in his determined effort to modernize—and indeed, to "Westernize"—the country.

Might Vietnam have ended differently if Nixon had stayed in office? Some supporters have contended that despite his public commitment to bring the war to a rapid end, he might have been less ready to withdraw all American forces from Vietnam early in 1975, still hoping for a way to save South Vietnam from a communist takeover.

Throughout his presidency, Nixon was gripped by the question of how history might remember him. What "footsteps" would he wind up leaving on "'the sands of time." Friends and advisors consistently worked to reassure him in this regard, and of course this was particularly true at the time of his resignation.

After delivering his televised farewell address from the Oval Office on the evening of August 8, 1974, Nixon returned to his residence in the thoughtful company of Henry Kissinger. As both men later recalled these moments, a grief-stricken Nixon asked Kissinger to pray with him, reflecting tearfully on the course of his life's challenges, and affirming that, whatever had happened, he had always tried "to do my best."

Kissinger resolutely reassured him that "history will remember you much kindlier than your contemporaries." Nixon's reply:

"Well, Henry.....It depends on who writes the history."

APPENDIX

The "Checkers" Speech

The Checkers Speech broke new ground in several ways. It was the first nationally televised speech, attracting the largest audience ever yet assembled for one address and rescuing Nixon's career not only by providing what some called a financial striptease" but by also focusing unprecedented attention on the speaker's personal and family life. The Nixon insisted on calling it "The Fund Speech," as it successfully addressed unsubstantiated charges concerning Nixon's financial life.

My Fellow Americans:

I come before you tonight as a candidate for the Vice Presidency and as a man whose honesty and integrity have been questioned.

Now, the usual political thing to do when charges are made against you is to either ignore them or to deny them without giving details. I believe we've had enough of that in the United States, particularly with the present administration in Washington, D.C. To me the office of the Vice Presidency of the United States is a great office and I feel that the people have got to have confidence in the integrity of the men who run for that office and who might obtain it.

I have a theory, too, that the best and only answer to a smear or to an honest misunderstanding of the facts is to tell the truth. And that's why I'm here tonight. I want to tell you my side of the case.

I am sure that you have read the charge and you've heard that I, Senator Nixon, took $18,000 from a group of my supporters.

Now, was that wrong? And let me say that it was wrong—I'm saying, incidentally, that it was wrong, not just illegal, because it isn't a question of whether it was legal or illegal, that isn't enough. The question is, was it morally wrong?

I say that it was morally wrong if any of that $18,000 went to Senator Nixon for my personal use. I say that it was morally wrong if it was secretly given and secretly handled. And I say that it was morally wrong if any of the contributors got special favors for the contributions that they made.

And now to answer those questions let me say this:

Not one cent of the $18,000 or any other money of that type ever went to me for my personal use. Every penny of it was used to pay for political expenses that I did not think should be charged to the taxpayers of the United States.

It was not a secret fund. As a matter of fact, when I was on *Meet the Press*—some of you may have seen it last Sunday—Peter Edson came up to me after the program and he said, "Dick, what about this fund we hear about?" And I said, "well, there's no secret about it. Go out and see Dana Smith, who was the administrator of the fund." And I gave him his address, and I said that you will find that the purpose of the fund simply was to defray political expenses that I did not feel should be charged to the Government.

And third, let me point out – and I want to make this particularly clear – that no contributor to this fund, no contributor to any of my campaigns, has ever received any consideration that he would not have received as an ordinary constituent. I just don't believe in that. And I can say that never, while I have been in the Senate of the United States, as far as the people that contributed to this fund are concerned, have I made a telephone call for them to an agency, or have I gone down to an agency in their behalf. And the records will show that, the records which are in the hands of the administration.

Well then, some of you will say, and rightly, "well, what did you use the fund for, Senator? Why did you have to have it?"

Let me tell you in just a word how a Senate office operates. First of all, a Senator gets $15,000 a year in salary. He gets enough money to pay for one trip a year, a round trip that is, for himself and his family between his home and Washington, D.C.

And then he gets an allowance to handle the people that work in his office, to handle his mail. And the allowance for my state of California is enough to hire thirteen people. And let me say, incidentally, that that allowance is not paid to the Senator—it's paid directly to the individuals that the Senator puts on his payroll. But all of these people and all of these allowances are for strictly official business. Business, for example, when a constituent writes in and wants you to go down to the Veterans Administration and get some information about his G.I. policy. Items of that type for example.

But there are other expenses which are not covered by the government. And I think I can best discuss those expenses by asking you some questions.

Do you think that when I or any other Senator makes a political speech, has it printed, should charge the printing of that speech and the mailing of that speech to the taxpayers? Do you think, for example, when I or any other Senator makes a trip to his home state to make a purely political speech, that the cost of that trip should be charged to the taxpayers? Do you think when a Senator makes political broadcasts or political television broadcasts, radio or television, that the expense of those broadcasts should be charged to the taxpayers?

Well, I know what your answer is. It is the same answer that audiences give me whenever I discuss this particular problem. The answer is no: the taxpayers shouldn't be required to finance items which are not official business but which are primarily political business.

Well then the question arises. You say, "well, how do you pay for these and how can you do it legally?" And there are several ways that it can be done, incidentally, and that it is done legally in the United States Senate and in the Congress.

The first way is to be a rich man. I don't happen to be a rich man so I couldn't use that one.

Another way that is used is to put your wife on the payroll. Let me say, incidentally, my opponent, my opposite number for the Vice Presidency on the Democratic ticket, does have his wife on the payroll, and has had her on his payroll for the ten years—the past ten years. Now just let me say this: that's his business, and I'm not critical of him for doing that. You will have to pass judgment on that particular point. But I have never done that for this reason. I have found that there are so many deserving stenographers and secretaries in Washington that needed the work that I just didn't feel it was right to put my wife on the payroll.

My wife's sitting over here. She's a wonderful stenographer. She used to teach stenography,and she used to teach shorthand in high school. That was when I met her. And I can tell you folks that she's worked many hours at night and many hours on Saturdays and Sundays in my office, and she's done a fine job. And I'm proud to say tonight that in the six years I've been in the House and the Senate of the United States, Pat Nixon has never been on the government payroll.

Well, there are other ways that these finances can be taken care of. Some who are lawyers, and I happen to be a lawyer, continue to practice law. But I haven't been able to do that. I'm so far away from California that I've been so busy with my senatorial work that I have not engaged in any legal practice.

And also, as far as law practice is concerned, it seemed to me that the relationship between an attorney and the client was so personal that you couldn't possibly represent a man as an attorney and then have an unbiased view when he presented his case to you in the event that he had one before the government.

And so I felt that the best way to handle these necessary political expenses of getting my message to the American people and the speeches I made, the speeches that I had printed, for the most part, concerned this one message—of exposing this administration, the communism in it, the corruption in it—the only way that I could do that was to accept the aid which people in my home state of California who contributed to my campaign, and who continued to make these contributions after I was elected were glad to make.

And let me say I am proud of the fact that not one of them has ever asked me for a special favor. I'm proud of the fact that not one of them has ever asked me to vote on a bill other than as my own conscience would dictate. And I am proud of the fact that the taxpayers, by subterfuge or otherwise, have never paid one dime for expenses which I thought were political and shouldn't be charged to the taxpayers.

Let me say, incidentally, that some of you may say, "Well, that's all right, Senator; that's your explanation, but have you got any proof?" And I'd like to tell you this evening that just about an hour ago we received an independent audit of this entire fund. I suggested to Governor Sherman Adams, who is the chief of staff of the Dwight Eisenhower campaign, that an independent audit and legal report be obtained. And I have that audit here in my hand. It's an audit made by the Price, Waterhouse & Co. firm, and the legal opinion by Gibson, Dunn & Crutcher, lawyers in Los Angeles, the biggest law firm, and incidentally, one of the best ones in Los Angeles.

I'm proud to be able to report to you tonight that this audit and this legal opinion is being forwarded to General Eisenhower. And I'd like to read to you the opinion that was prepared by Gibson, Dunn & Crutcher, and based on all the pertinent laws and statutes, together with the audit report prepared by the certified public accountant:

> "It is our conclusion that Senator Nixon did not obtain any financial gain from the collection and disbursement of the fund by Dana Smith; that Senator Nixon did not violate any Federal or state law by reason of the operation of the fund, and that neither the portion of the fund paid by Dana Smith directly to third persons nor the portion paid to Senator Nixon to reimburse him for designated office expenses constituted income to the Senator which was either reportable or taxable as income under applicable tax laws. Signed, Gibson, Dunn & Crutcher, by Alma H. Conway."

Now that, my friends, is not Nixon speaking, but that's an independent audit which was requested because I want the American people to know all the facts and I'm not afraid of having independent people go in and check the facts, and that is exactly what they did.

But then I realize that there are still some who may say, and rightly so, and let me say that I recognize that some will continue to smear regardless of what the truth may be, but that there has been understandably some honest misunderstanding on this matter, and there's some that will say: "Well, maybe you were able, Senator, to fake this thing. How can we believe what you say? After all, is there a possibility that maybe you got some sums in cash? Is there a possibility that you may have feathered your own nest?"

And so now what I am going to do—and incidentally, this is unprecedented in the history of American politics—I am going at this time to give this television and radio audience a complete financial history: Everything I've earned, everything I've spent, everything I owe. And I want you to know the facts. I'll have to start early.

I was born in 1913. Our family was one of modest circumstances and most of my early life was spent in a store out in East Whittier. It was a grocery store—one of those family enterprises. The only reason we were able to make it go was because my mother and dad had five boys and we all worked in the store.

I worked my way through college, and to a great extent, through law school. And then, in 1940, probably the best thing that ever happened to me happened, I married Pat—who is sitting over here. We had a rather difficult time after we were married, like so many of the young couples who may be listening to us. I practiced law; she continued to teach school.

Then in 1942 I went into the service. Let me say that my service record was not a particularly unusual one. I went to the South Pacific. I guess I'm entitled to a couple of battle stars. I got a couple of letters of commendation but I was just there when the bombs were falling and then I returned. I returned to the United States and in 1946 I ran for the Congress.

When we came out of the war, Pat and I – Pat, during the war, had worked as a stenographer, and in a bank, and as an economist for a government agency – and when we came out the total of our savings from both my law practice, her teaching, and all the time that I was in the war, the total for that entire period was just a little less than $10,000. Every cent of that, incidentally, was in government bonds. Well, that's where we start when I go into politics.

Now what I've I earned since I went into politics? Well, here it is—I jotted it down. Let me read the notes.

First of all, I've had my salary as a Congressman, and as a Senator. Second, I have received a total in this past six years of $1600 from estates which were in my law firm at the time that I severed my connection with it. And, incidentally, as I said before, I have not engaged in any legal practice and have not accepted any fees from business that came to the firm after I went into politics. I have made an average of approximately $1500 a year from nonpolitical speaking engagements and lectures. And then, fortunately, we've inherited a little money. Pat sold her interest in her father's estate for $3,000 and I inherited $1500 from my grandfather.

We live rather modestly. For four years we lived in an apartment in Park Fairfax, in Alexandria, Virginia. The rent was $80.00 a month. And we saved for the time that we could buy a house.

Now, that was what we took in. What did we do with this money? What do we have today to show for it? This will surprise you because it is so little, I suppose, as standards generally go, of people in public life.

First of all, we've got a house in Washington which cost $41,000 and on which we owe $20,000. We have a house in Whittier, California, which cost $13,000 and on which we owe $3000. My folks are living there at the present time.

I have just $4,000 in life insurance, plus my G.I. policy which I've never been able to convert, and which will run out in two years. I have no life insurance whatever on Pat. I have no life insurance on our two youngsters, Tricia and Julie. I own a 1950 Oldsmobile car. We have our furniture. We have no stocks and bonds of any type. We have no interest of any kind, direct or indirect, in any business.

Now, that's what we have. What do we owe? Well, in addition to the mortgage, the $20,000 mortgage on the house in Washington, the $10,000 one on the house in Whittier, I owe $4,500 to the Riggs Bank in Washington, D.C. with interest 4.5 percent.

I owe $3,500 to my parents and the interest on that loan which I pay regularly, because it's the part of the savings they made through the years they were working so hard, I pay regularly 4 per cent interest. And then I have a $500 loan which I have on my life insurance.

Well, that's about it. That's what we have, and that's what we owe. It isn't very much but Pat and I have the satisfaction that every dime that we've got is honestly ours. I should say this—that Pat doesn't have a mink coat, but she does have a respectable Republican cloth coat. And I always tell her that she'd look good in anything.

One other thing I probably should tell you, because if I don't, they'll probably be saying this about me too. We did get something – a gift – after the election. A man down in Texas heard Pat on the radio mention the fact that our two youngsters would like to have a dog. And believe it or not, the day before we left on this campaign trip, we got a message from the Union Station in Baltimore saying they had a package for us. We went down to get it. You know what it was? It was a little cocker spaniel dog in a crate that he'd sent all the way from Texas. Black and white, spotted. And our little girl-Tricia, the six-year old, named it Checkers. And you know, the kids, like all kids, love the dog. And I just want to say this right now, that regardless of what they say about it, we're gonna keep him.

It isn't easy to come before a nation-wide audience and air your life as I've done. But I want to say some things before I conclude that I think most of you will agree on.

Mr. Mitchell, the chairman of the Democratic National Committee, made the statement that if a man couldn't afford to be in the United States Senate, he shouldn't run for the Senate. And I just want to make my position clear. I don't agree with Mr. Mitchell when he says that only a rich man should serve his government in the United States Senate or in the Congress. I don't believe that represents the thinking of the Democratic Party, and I know that it doesn't represent the thinking of the Republican Party

I believe that it's fine that a man like Governor Stevenson, who inherited a fortune from his father, can run for President. But I also feel that it's essential in this country of ours that a man of modest means can also run for President. Because, you know, remember Abraham Lincoln, you remember what he said: "God must have loved the common people – he made so many of them."

And now I'm going to suggest some courses of conduct. First of all, you have read in the papers about other funds now. Mr. Stevenson, apparently, had a couple, one of them in which a group of business people paid and helped to supplement the salaries of state employees. Here is where the money went directly into their pockets.

And I think that what Mr. Stevenson should do should be to come before the American people as I have, give the names of the people that have contributed to that fund; give the names of the people who put this money into their pockets at the same time that they were receiving money from their state government, and see what favors, if any, they gave out for that. I don't condemn Mr. Stevenson for what he did. But until the facts are in, there is a doubt that will be raised.

And as far as Mr. Sparkman is concerned, I would suggest the same thing. He's had his wife on the payroll. I don't condemn him for that. But I think that he should come before the American people and indicate what outside sources of income he has had.

I would suggest that under the circumstances both Mr. Sparkman and Mr. Stevenson should come before the American people as I have and make a complete financial statement as to their financial history. And if they don't, it will be an admission that they have something to hide. And I think that you will agree with me.

Because, folks, remember, a man that's to be President of the United States, a man that's to be Vice President of the United States, must have the confidence of all the people. And that's why I'm doing what I'm doing, and that's why I suggest that Mr. Stevenson and Mr. Sparkman, since they are under attack, should do what they're [I am] doing.

Now, let me say this. I know that this is not the last of the smears. In spite of my explanation tonight, other smears will be made; others have been made in the past. And the purpose of the smears, I know, is this – to silence me, to make me let up.

Well, they just don't know who they're dealing with. I'm going l tell you this: I remember in the dark days of the Hiss case, some of the same columnists, some of the same radio commentators who are attacking me now and misrepresenting my position, were violently opposing me at the time I was after Alger Hiss. But I continued to fight because I knew I was right. And I can say to this great television and radio audience that I have no apologies to the American people for my part in putting Alger Hiss where he is today. And as far as this is concerned, I intend to continue the fight.

Why do I feel so deeply? Why do I feel that in spite of the smears, the misunderstandings, the necessity for a man to come up here and bare his soul as I have? Why is it necessary for me to continue this fight?

And I want to tell you why. Because, you see, I love my country. And I think my country is in danger. And I think that the only man that can save America at this time is the man that's running for President on my ticket: Dwight Eisenhower.

You say, "why do I think it's in danger?" and I say, look at the record. Seven years of the Truman-Acheson Administration and what's happened? 600 million people lost to the Communists, and a war in Korea in which we have lost 117,000 American casualties.And I say to all of you that a policy that results in a loss of six hundred million people to the Communists and a war which costs us 117,000 American casualties isn't good enough for America.

And I say that those in the State Department that made the mistakes which caused that war and which resulted in those losses should be kicked out of the State Department just as fast as we can get 'em out of there.

And let me say that I know Mr. Stevenson won't do that, because he defends the Truman policy; and I know that Dwight Eisenhower will do that, and that he will give America the leadership that it needs.

Take the problem of corruption. You've read about the mess in Washington. Mr. Stevenson can't clean it up because he was picked by the man, Truman, under whose administration the mess was made. You wouldn't trust a man who made the mess to clean it up—that's Truman. And by the same token you can't trust the man who was picked by the man that made the mess to clean it up—and that's Stevenson.

And so I say, Eisenhower, who owes nothing to Truman, nothing to the big city bosses, he is the man that can clean up the mess in Washington.

Take Communism. I say that as far as that subject is concerned, the danger is great to America. In the Hiss case they got the secrets which enabled them to break the American secret State Department code. They got secrets in the atomic bomb case which enabled them to get the secret of the atomic bomb, five years before they would have gotten it by their own devices.

And I say that any man who called the Alger Hiss case a "red herring" isn't fit to be President of the United States. I say that a man who, like Mr. Stevenson has pooh-poohed and ridiculed the Communist threat in the United States, he said that they are phantoms among ourselves. He has accused us that have attempted to expose the Communists of looking for Communists in the Bureau of Fisheries and Wildlife. I say that a man who says that isn't qualified to be President of the United States. And I say that the only man who can lead us in this fight to rid the Government of both those who are Communists and those who have corrupted this Government is Eisenhower, because Eisenhower, you can be sure, recognizes the problem and he knows how to deal with it.

Now let me say that, finally, this evening I want to read to you just briefly excerpts from a letter which I received, a letter which, after all this is over, no one can take away from us. It reads as follows:

> "Dear Senator Nixon:
>
> Since I'm only 19 years of age I can't vote in this Presidential election. But believe me, if I could, you and General Eisenhower would certainly get my vote. My husband is in the Fleet Marines in Korea. He's a corpsman on the front lines and we have a two-month-old son he's never seen. And I feel confident that with great Americans like you and General Eisenhower in the White House, lonely Americans like myself will be united with their loved ones now in Korea.
>
> I only pray to God that you won't be too late. Enclosed is a small check to help you in your campaign. Living on $85 a month it is all I can afford at present. But let me know what else I can do."
>
> Folks, it's a check for $10.00, and it's one that I will never cash.

And just let me say this. We hear a lot about prosperity these days. But I say, why can't we have prosperity built on peace, rather than prosperity built on war? Why can't we have prosperity and an honest government in Washington, D.C., at the same time. Believe me, we can. And Eisenhower is the man that can lead this crusade to bring us that kind of prosperity.

And, now, finally, I know that you wonder whether or not I am going to stay on the Republican ticket or resign.

Let me say this: I don't believe that I ought to quit because I am not a quitter. And, incidentally, Pat's not a quitter. After all, her name was Patricia Ryan and she was born on St. Patrick's Day, and you know the Irish never quit.

But the decision, my friends, is not mine. I would do nothing that would harm the possibilities of Dwight Eisenhower to become President of the United States. And for that reason, I am submitting to the Republican National Committee tonight through this television broadcast the decision which it is theirs to make. Let them decide whether my position on the ticket will help or hurt. And I am going to ask you to help them decide.

Wire and write the Republican National Committee whether you think I should stay on or whether I should get off. And whatever their decision is, I will abide by it.

But just let me say this last word. Regardless of what happens I'm going to continue this fight. I'm going to campaign up and down in America until we drive the crooks and the Communists and those that defend them out of Washington. And remember, folks, Eisenhower is a great man. Believe me. He's a great man. And a vote for Eisenhower is a vote for what's good for America.

Commencement Address, Lafayette College, June 7, 1956

The Lafayette College Speech reflected Nixon's continuing effort, as the 1956 election approached, to reverse his "hatchet" man image, re-establish his serious policy credentials (especially in international affairs), and keep his place as President Eisenhower's running mate, despite a concerted effort by some Republicans to replace him and despite the President's own uncertainty.

I was tempted in preparing my remarks for this occasion to discuss at length the economic prospects for the years ahead. We are fortunate to be living in a period when, for the first time in a quarter of a century, we have had three consecutive years of unparalleled prosperity. The college graduates of 1956 will find available to them the most jobs at the highest wages in the nation's history. And it would be fascinating indeed to explore the almost limitless possibilities for expansion of the American economy during the years ahead, as we begin to harness the new sources of energy which our scientists have untapped.

Tonight, however, I believe there is a subject of greater importance to this graduating class and to the nation. I refer to the titanic struggle between two opposing concepts of life in which we are engaged.

The next few years will determine whether we can live in peace and at the same time avoid surrender. And that question will be answered by how well we are able to meet and defeat the changing tactics of the dictatorial forces which threaten the free world.

From the end of World War II to the death of Stalin in 1953, our problem was a relatively simple one. Communist leaders all over the world used open threats of force coupled with thinly-veiled support of revolutionary and subversive movements in countries designed for conquest. These actions of bluster and abuse inevitably drove the free world together in self-defense. Then came the death of Stalin and the "New Look" in Communist foreign relations. The leaders of the Soviet Union invited the rest of the world to a period of peaceful co-existence. In doing so they seemed to abandon their previous tough line and they have even repudiated some of the excesses of past regimes.

This change of tactics has understandably created considerable confusion in the non-Communist world. I think there will be little dissent from the conclusion that in view of the record of the men in the Kremlin, the lines of military and diplomatic policy that we have hammered out over the past 10 years must continue to govern our conduct at this time.

But is this the whole answer? Do we stand pat and leave all the initiative to the other camp? Do we act as if nothing has happened in the three years since Stalin died?

I answer these questions by saying that we could make no greater mistake than to rest on our oars and to ignore the "New Look" in Soviet diplomacy. If it is made to appear that our primary concern is military hardware, we may find ourselves isolated in a world that has been convinced by the traveling salesmen of the Soviet Union selling other products. What we face today is a new line which could be far more dangerous in the long run than the Stalin line of bluster and brute force. It is basically a war for men's minds, a struggle for their allegiance, an effort to win them peacefully to the Soviet Camp.

In this struggle, ideas—not guns or aircraft—are the weapons. In this war, our armies wear the university cap and gown—not the uniform of the soldier. Books and pamphlets, rather than tanks and battleships, will be decisive in this contest.

One of the major reasons for the change in Soviet policy now becomes apparent. It was obvious to the successors of Stalin that they could not sell their new line so long as people remembered slave labor camps, mass purges, and the ever-present terror of the secret police. Yet, to the outside world, there would appear to be a break with the past and a writing off of the handicaps derived from more than thirty years of terror. And the "New Look" was sufficiently appealing in contrast to the old that there was every chance of selling this policy to uncommitted nations, and of breaking off one by one those who had allied together in a common policy defense.

In the cold light of history, it seems fantastic that a nation with the Soviet record of terror and aggression could hope to make widespread gains by announcing a simple change of policy. At the least, one would expect that all non-Communist countries would adopt a policy of watchful waiting and not make any shift of program until the "New Look" had been tried for five to ten years. Unfortunately, this is not the case. We must recognize that there are powerful assets which work to the benefit of the Soviet in this contest. Unless we examine them and face them realistically, we may well lose out in the battle for men's minds.

First, let us see what is at stake. Approximately 600 million people live in the so-called "uncommitted" or "neutral" nations. It is easy to see that the world struggle will be determined by what happens to these people. On the basis of my travels through most of this part of the world, may I tell you what I believe the people in the uncommitted nations want, and contrast the Communist appeal with our own.

First, there is the desire for peace throughout the world, a desire which is particularly strong in the nations newly freed from colonial ties. This is not merely negative in the sense of war weariness or fear; it is often something much more positive. They wish the time and freedom to build their countries: economically, politically, and culturally.

To such nations, the Communist world talks and promises peace. It appears to respect their desire for neutrality. By contrast, we often seem to be talking war and military alliances. [I] Do not say that these impressions are correct, but they are more widespread and sincerely held than we often realize.

Second, there is the understandable desire for economic progress in nations less developed than those in the West. To these nations, the Soviet Union holds up the example of its own dramatic industrial progress under Communism. On the other hand, the almost unbelievable prosperity of the United States appears to many of these nations as a goal impossible of attainment.

Third, there is the desire for recognition, prestige, and independence. In much of Asia and Africa, strong resentments have been built up against Western nations because of past or present colonial and imperialistic policies. Often, there is the deep hurt that springs from real or imagined racial discrimination. Here we find that there is a fear of what they term "cultural imperialism," an effort by the West to dominate the thinking of other nations rather than to respect their cultures and religions on an equal basis with ours.

And here again the Soviet has been adroit in recognizing this desire. Compare, for example, the tactics of Bulganin and Khrushchev in dealing with the peoples of the Far East, and their tactics in Great Britain.

A fourth point to note is the attitude of many peoples toward material things in contrast to the intellectual and the spiritual. This is difficult to express accurately. In one sense, all peoples are concerned with economic and material problems. They must produce to live. Yet, at the same time, there are often profound differences in the relative place assigned to these activities. In many areas of the world, a place of honor is given to leaders in the arts and intellectual fields, and in religious activities. The intellectual is not dismissed as an egghead. The artist is not called a long-hair. The minister of religion is not considered an impractical idealist.

Here again, we find that many peoples think that we in America are too materialistic to have such ideals. We are considered anti-intellectual, deficient in culture, superficial in religion. Again, I am not passing judgement on the truth or falsity of these charges. The important point is that they are widely believed. And what is truly amazing is this—that the apostles of Communism can parade as [exponents] of the very ideals that they accuse us of neglecting when their own philosophy is the ultimate in materialism and the antithesis of religion.

But we find again how cleverly they present their case. They point out that the scientist and the intellectual is held in high esteem in the Soviet Union. Artists and writers are among the highest paid and most honored citizens in their regime. Even the persecution of religion is played down by the claim that worship is free, and that only political activities of the Churches are suppressed.

We now come to the basic question: What should our policy be in the light of the new Soviet tactics? We must, of course, continue to maintain adequate military strength at home and we must try to keep alive our vital alliances abroad We must continue our programs of economic assistance, and avoid, if we can, the possibility that less-developed nations will be forced to become economic satellites of the Soviet Union. But our military and economic programs, essential as they are, may not prove to be the most important elements in this battle. Of this we can be sure: the uncommitted nations are not going to be frightened into alliances with the West by military power, nor can their allegiance be purchased by dollars. What will probably be decisive in this struggle is not how much each side does, but how it is done. That is why we must, at whatever cost, place additional emphasis on developing the kind of ideological program which is designed to win the minds and hearts of men.

Before I discuss details of such a program, may I suggest one fundamental condition that can make the difference between success and failure: Whatever we do, we must deal with other people as our moral and spiritual equals. Nothing is more infuriating, or more likely, to make our program fail than a boastful or condescending attitude on our part. It is dangerous to parade our material wealth or economic achievement. This may merely create envy, rather than admiration, on the part of other peoples.

In a sense, we must deal with other nations with the tact, humility, and friendliness of missionaries. Indeed, we could learn a great deal in our foreign relations by studying the attitudes and methods of the Christian missionaries who have won friends throughout the world. They came to help the nations to which they were sent. They learned their languages and customs. By taking literally the truth that all men are brothers under God, they were accepted into families and homes of distant peoples. Once we have this attitude, our task is to convince others that democracy and freedom, and all the rights and privileges we hold sacred, are better for them than is the Soviet way of life. It is not enough to denounce or expose Communism. We must show that we have a better alternative. We do not do this by parading our superior material standard of living. It is the total pattern of life that must prevail—not merely one phase of it.

May I make one point clear at this time? There is no question but that we have the better case to sell, because basically we are on the right side. The side of freedom and justice, of belief in God against the forces of slavery, injustice and atheistic materialism. Ours is the truly revolutionary dynamic idea. It is the Communist idea which is repressive and reactionary.

How do we get our message across? I believe that often, too much reliance is placed upon the effectiveness of bombarding the uncommitted countries with radio broadcasts, motion pictures, and press releases which present the American viewpoint. These programs are important and necessary. But, in the long run, I believe there are others which are most effective.

May I emphasize first the overwhelming importance of expanding our program for exchange of persons. This includes high school youngsters who spend a year living with American families and going to our schools, college and university students who get their degrees in American schools, and the leaders program under which each week, 50 or more foreign visitors—leaders in business, government, labor, and education—come to the United States as guests of our government to talk with Americans who are in the same field as theirs. In this way, our guests learn about us firsthand, correcting false impressions they may have had about us. It is particularly important that we expand this program in countries newly released from colonial status. Here the need for trained leaders is often the greatest. Many times, students will graduate from a university and almost immediately take a high political position in their native lands.

From a long-range point of view, we can gain immensely by programs of this nature. For the cost of one large bomber, we can make friendships that will benefit the free world for generations to come. President Eisenhower's brilliant proposal that American educational institutions and foundations aid in expanding educational opportunities throughout the world is in line with this approach. If the free world can teach the leaders of tomorrow in areas that may well dominate tomorrow's world, we need not fear the contest between Communism and freedom.

There are those, of course, who may point out the fact that many of those who today oppose Western policies were trained in Western universities. But they oppose us because we taught them ideals of freedom while we were keeping their lands in colonial bondage. Now that great areas of the world are free from colonialism, we have a good chance to win back the friendship and loyalty of leaders of these lands.

In addition to government-sponsored activities, it is important that every American who goes abroad or who deals with foreign guests in our own land realizes that he is an ambassador representing our nation. All of us must try to be sensitive, understanding, and helpful. Arrogance and boastfulness make enemies, not friends. And particularly, we must appreciate the high place given to intellectual and spiritual values in many areas of the world. This places a tremendous responsibility upon our tourists and business visitors, upon the exporters of motion pictures and books—indeed, upon anyone who is likely to be taken as a representative of our way of life.

I was reading an article the other day that showed the importance of these attitudes. It concerned the great atomic scientist, Bruno Pontecorvo, who left Great Britain to devote his genius to Soviet atomic research. One of the important reasons for his defection, according to his colleagues, was the fact that he thought he would have more honor, prestige, and even greater freedom of research in the Soviet Union. Likewise, many of the scientists who got caught in the Soviet espionage network in the United

States, Canada, and Great Britain, were partially influenced at least by the feeling that they were not sufficiently appreciated in the free world. The world of tomorrow belongs to the nations that lead in scientific research and technical skill. We shall pay a great price if we fall behind in this contest.

In discussing our need to win the war for men's minds, I have said little about direct contacts with the people behind the Iron Curtain. Today we can have such contacts almost for the asking. If the present trend continues in the Soviet Union and in many satellite countries, it will be possible to meet broadly with these peoples, to exchange ideas, to compare our respective ways of life.

Many of my fellow Americans are rather skeptical about this new move. They suspect, with some justification, a hidden trick-possibly a device to make Communism respectable and to discourage the people held in submission by Red armies. I do not fully share this point of view. I think that the explosive power of freedom is greater than the combined effect of all the atomic and hydrogen weapons in the world today.

Whatever be the motives behind these new moves, I think that in the long run, the cause of freedom will be served by breaking through the Iron Curtain wherever an opportunity is presented. The task ahead of us is a task for all the American people, and not government alone. In time of war, we are prepared to risk our lives serving with the armed forces of our country.

But the war for men's minds is a real war and just as important as the struggle of armies, navies, and air forces. You in the academic world are particularly fitted to serve in this contest. May I suggest that you graduates and you of the faculty give thought to the part that you can play.

On an even broader sphere, I hope that the learned societies of the United States with their counterparts in other free nations will devote time and energy to extend their study to this great struggle for allegiance. Jointly, you should embark upon a peaceful crusade for freedom. Some should volunteer for service abroad, just as soldiers volunteer for special missions.

The best thought of our best minds should be given to this burning problem. It was once said that "you shall know the truth and the truth shall make you free." This challenge has echoed through the ages. It is as valid today as it was when it was uttered more than nineteen centuries ago.

We believe in truth and in the power of truth. We believe in such basic truths as man's equality under God, the dignity of man, the rights of each individual to live his life in peace, the sacredness of law, the benefits of political freedom including the freedoms guaranteed in our Bill of Rights. These truths are the great heritage of mankind. We are confident that they will prevail. And it is the task of this generation to make sure that our confidence is not misplaced and that all Americans will rise to the challenge that faces us.

Address to the English-Speaking Union, Guildhall, London, November 26, 1958

The London Guildhall Address was one that Nixon came to see as one of his best speeches, a text that he often urged his speechwriters to read and reread, referring especially to the way in he found just the right quotation from William Pitt to underscore his message to the British people as they moved into a new era of international relationships.

In the six years in which I have had the honor of serving as Vice President of the United States, it has been my privilege to visit many countries and to participate in many significant events. I can assure you that no occasion in that period will live more indelibly in my memory than the dedication of the American Chapel at St. Paul's which I attended this morning and the gathering in this historic hall which I am privileged to address this evening.

The meeting of the English Speaking Union dramatizes the enduring character of the friendship and alliance of our two countries. The activities of this organization have been most vital in cementing our bonds of comradeship.

I consider it a particular privilege to pay tribute to the thoughtful and inspiring leadership of His Royal Highness, Prince Philip, who has spared no sacrifices in this dedicated work. His recent visit to Canada was only one of many activities which indicate his vital interest. You may all be justly proud, not only of the contribution you have made to better understanding between our two countries, but also the even greater work of building an enduring basis of friendship among all English-speaking peoples.

The dedication at St. Paul's this morning dramatizes the unity you have worked so hard to achieve. It was symbolic of the enduring ties that bind us. It brought to mind the dramatic events of earlier and more trying days—the magnificent leadership and the great sacrifices that made possible our victory in the Second World War.

Our thoughts went back to our great national leaders, Sir Winston Churchill and President Roosevelt, working together in intimate harmony. They will receive the ungrudging tribute of history for their capacity to marshal the forces of democracy. Our thoughts turned also to our incomparable Generals and Admirals—Eisenhower and Montgomery, Cunningham and King. They were than brilliant strategists and commanders. Because of their unwavering devotion to the concept that military ingenuity must be combined with recognition of civilian authority, they rank indeed among the great military leaders of all times.

But above all, today, we honored brave men—whose names are legion and whose sacrifice, in can never adequately be repaid. British and American, farmers and laborers, from cities and countryside, from offices and classrooms—these were the men who made possible our victory the greatest war in history. Many events of that war will be forgotten as we turn our eyes to other tasks, but their deeds will live forever. They bequeathed to us a spirit, a sentiment, a national memory that will never fail to capture our admiration as we move side by side in the path of friendship and alliance.

THE UNFINISHED WORK

As Abraham Lincoln said at Gettysburg, "the world will little note nor long remember what we say here, but it can never forget what they did here. It is for us, the living, rather to be dedicated here to the unfinished work which they who fought here have thus far so nobly advanced."

What is the unfinished work they leave for our generation? I believe that two American Presidents speaking in this same Guildhall have simply, but, eloquently, answered that question. Woodrow Wilson on December 28, 1918, said "the peoples of the world want peace and they want it now, not merely by conquest of arms, but by agreement of mind."

And Dwight D. Eisenhower, twenty-seven years later on July 12, 1945, said, to preserve his freedom of worship, his equality before law, his liberty to speak and act as he sees fit subject only to provisions that he trespass not upon similar rights of others, a Londoner will fight. So will a citizen of Abilene."

To preserve freedom, to keep the peace, not only for themselves but for all people—this, then, is the cause for which the brave men we honored today gave their lives. It is the challenge and opportunity of our generation to further the ultimate realization of this noblest goal of mankind.

Let us examine the policies we should follow if this goal is to be attained. We begin by recognizing that the Free World must be militarily stronger than any potential aggressor. The existence of our military strength and our determination and ability to maintain it are the basic elements without which the objectives we seek would in and be impossible to realize. But we recognize that military strength of itself will not keep peace unless it is combined with a wise and judicious diplomatic policy.

Let us see what some of the guidelines for our policy should be. We must retain the armed strength needed for security in a troubled world, but we should speak with the calm assurance of those who are not afraid. We know that to the extent the law of the jungle prevails in any area of the world, weakness and indecision lead to disaster. Yet firmness is not and should not be arrogance. We will shun assurances based merely upon up naive hope or even self-deception. But we must never tire in our search for enforceable agreements which will reduce tension. We know that little is lost by discussion, but that all may be lost by war. Yet even in our tireless striving for peace, we must always be prepared to say that freedom and the rights of man are even more ultimate values.

Above all, our policies must represent the best thinking the Free World can produce. We are indeed fortunate in the fact that in men like Macmillan and de Gaulle, Adenauer and Spaak, Fanfani and Eisenhower, we have the kind of dedicated and experienced leadership which is superbly qualified for the difficult task of keeping the peace with honor for the Free World.

PRIME MINISTER PRAISED

In this connection, I wish to pay special tribute to your Prime Minister for his initiative in developing the enlightened concept of interdependence which has proved so useful in bringing about closer understanding between our two nations and which points the way for improving consultation and cooperation among all the countries in the Free World. If the struggles for peace and freedom were to be decided solely by the adequacy of our military strength and by the quality of our diplomacy, we could look to the future with justifiable confidence as to the prospects for our eventual success.

But we must recognize that this is only one phase of the struggle. Our military strength and our diplomatic policies are designed to avoid a war we might otherwise have to fight in the future. We must not overlook the fact that other policies must be designed to avoid losing the non-military battle which has already begun, and which is being waged in many areas of the world today.

Let us examine the battleground where this conflict is taking place—in Asia, in the Near East, in Africa, and in parts of Latin America. A great revolution is taking place among the people in these areas of the world. What I refer to is not a military or political revolt, but the revolution of peoples' expectations—the assertion of all peoples of their claim to a greater share of this world's goods. Millions of people in these newly developing nations are determined to break the bonds of wretchedness and poverty that have enslaved them through the centuries. They wish to achieve in this very generation a decisive breakthrough in the struggle against -misery and disease.

PROGRESS AND FREEDOM

They would prefer to attain these objectives and retain their freedom. But we must make [no] mistake about it—if they believe they are offered no other choice, they will choose progress even without freedom. What is their choice?

On the one hand, they now have the example of the Soviet Union and the Communist satellites. Here is a pattern that promises quick results. Thousands of leaders of these countries are being invited to visit the Soviet Union to see the very real changes accomplished in the 40 years since the Communist Revolution. It is not an adequate answer to this challenge to cite the far higher material standards in most Western nations.

To the newly developing nations of the world, this is not the point. They are not particularly impressed by achievements primarily accomplished in the century of the Industrial Revolution. They are far more interested in what can be accomplished in the last half of the 20th century. What must be made clear and unmistakable for all the world to see is that free peoples can compete with and surpass totalitarian nations in producing economic progress. No people in the world today should be forced to choose between bread and freedom. To shape the world of tomorrow in a pattern compatible with freedom and human rights, we must all take our part in a great offensive against the evils of poverty, disease and misery.

We cannot, for example, afford to allow the free government of India to fail in its heroic effort to produce economic progress and retain freedom at the same time. We need to apply in this field the same determination, willingness and cooperation which enabled us to build the military strength which deters aggression today.

We must not be miserly, small-minded and negative in our approach to this problem. And while it is wrong to favor change solely because it is change, it is worse blindly to insist that we have nothing better to offer than maintaining the status quo. We must associate ourselves with the decent aspirations of people everywhere for the better life to which they are entitled.

Just a few weeks ago, Premier Khrushchev promised his people a revolution in living standards within the next 12 years. He claimed that the Communist system would overtake and surpass, the economies of the Western World. We should be happy that such claims have been made. We would be eager to match the Soviet leaders in putting less emphasis upon armies, military research and the costly lethal weapons of modern warfare and more stress upon better housing, food, clothing and the other necessities for a good life. If Mr. Khrushchev wishes to consider these steps a form of competition or contest, I am sure that all of us would be delighted to accept the challenge. In such a contest no one could really lose. The world would be infinitely better off if man's energies were used for the welfare of families rather than the building of armies.

BROADEN COMPETITION

But our answer to the Soviet challenge should not stop here. We say, broaden this competition and include the spiritual and cultural values that have distinguished our civilization. Material achievements, while necessary, do not meet the deeper needs of mankind. Man needs the higher freedoms—freedom to know, to debate freely, to write and express his views. He needs the freedom that law and justice guarantee to every individual so that neither privilege nor power may make any man subservient before the law. He wants the freedom to travel and to learn from other peoples and cultures. He wants freedom of worship.

To us, these are the most precious aspects of our civilization. We would be happy if others were to compete in this sphere and try to surpass our achievements. The Free World is too often made to appear to be relying on our superior military power and economic strength. It is not worthy of those with the heritage of freedom we share to appear to be resting our case on materialism alone.

I know of no better example to illustrate the point I am trying to make than through an analysis of that much-maligned institution, British Colonialism. It is understandable in view of the surging rise of nationalism that we have heard all that is bad and little that is good about colonialism in the past few years. Colonialism has had its faults, but it also has had its virtues. I speak from some knowledge on this subject. I have visited 12 countries which at one time or another have passed through the status of British Colonialism.

COLONIAL POLICY

I have known personally and admired the dedicated and effective work of your superb colonial administrators. You can indeed be proud of the contributions that have been made by men like Grantham in Hong Kong, Templer in Kuala Lumpur, MacDonald in Singapore, Crawford in Uganda, and Arden-Clark in Ghana.

Let us examine some of the benefits British colonial policy has produced in the areas in which it has operated. It brought the military strength which provided the security from external attack. It brought in many areas the technical training which assured economic progress. But more important than either of these. it brought the great ideas which provided the basis for progress in the future—ideas which will live on for generations after the nations concerned have acquired the independent status for which an enlightened policy has prepared them. The common law, the parliament, the English language, freedom of speech, assembly, press and religion—these are the institutions which are the legacy of the British people in lands throughout the world.

And so today let us never forget that in the momentous struggle in which we are engaged, [one] major advantage is not in the strength of our arms or even the productivity of our factories. It is in the he quality and power of the great ideals our of freedom which have inspired men through the ages.

Our responsibility then is clear. Here is a cause worthy of the descendants of brave men and women who crossed boundless oceans and settled in every area of the globe. Once again we must venture forth not to seek untilled lands, but rather to bring encouragement, aid, guidance and partnership to those peoples who want to live in freedom and decent prosperity. We come to them as friends, as brothers in a shrinking world. We do not seek to impose upon them our economic system or our culture. It is theirs to choose the path to the future. But it is our responsibility to see that this choice is an informed one and a free one. Let it never be said that because of our failure to present adequately the aims and ideals of freedom others chose the often-irreversible path of dictatorship.

Let us speak less of the threat of Communism and more of the promise of freedom. Let us adopt as our primary objective not the defeat of Communism but the victory of plenty over want, of health over disease, of freedom over tyranny.

DAWN OF A NEW WORLD

With such a goal, we shall give the lie to those who proclaim that we are witnessing the twilight of a dying western civilization. Rather, we shall see the onset of a glorious dawn of a new world, based on the immortal ideals for which men have sacrificed their lives through the ages. In this very hall, a century and a half ago an English Prime Minister gave a brief address that has been ranked by Lord Curzon as one of the indisputable masterpieces of English eloquence. [After the news of Nelson's glorious victory, at 53 Trafalgar] William Pitt was toasted as "the saviour of Europe." He responded in these words: "I return you many thanks for the honor you have done me. But Europe is not to be saved by any single man. England has saved herself by her exertions, and will, as I trust, save Europe by her example."

Here is a challenge worthy of the brave men we honored today. May we, the English-speaking peoples, proud in the heritage we share, join with the friends of freedom everywhere and by our example save the cause of peace and freedom for the world.

* * *

The 1960 Election Results

One of Nixon's best admired moments (especially in more recent years) came at the end of his time as the U.S. Vice President when he was the presiding officer at the Joint Session of the Congress at which the electoral votes in the 1960 presidential election were officially counted. It became his duty to announce the results of a contest which he had lost to John F. Kennedy by the narrowest-imaginable margin He had been was widely advised to contest the result, given apparent irregularities in some voting tabulations, but he rejected that course, not only because it would cast him as "sore loser" but also because it would take some time and undermine national and international confidence in the concept of democratic elections.

Statement to a Joint Session of Congress, January 6, 1961

Mr. Speaker, since this is somewhat an unprecedented situation, I would like to ask permission to impose upon the time of the members of this Congress to make a statement which is somewhat unprecedented.

I promise to be brief. I shall be guided by the one-minute rule of the House rather than the unlimited time rule that prevails in the Senate.

This is the first time in 100 years that a candidate for the Presidency announced the result of an election in which he was defeated and announced the victory of his opponent. I do not think that we could have a more striking and eloquent example of the stability of our constitutional system, and of the proud tradition of the American people of developing, and respecting, and honoring institutions of self-government.

In our campaigns, no matter how hard-fought they may be, no matter how close the election may turn out to be, those who lose accept the verdict, and support those who win.

And I would like to add that, having served now in government for 14 years, a period which began in the House just 14 years ago, almost to the day, which continued with two years in the Senate and eight years as Vice President, as I complete that 14-year period it is indeed a very great honor for me to extend to my colleagues in the House and Senate on both sides of the aisle who have been elected, to extend to John F. Kennedy and Lyndon Johnson, who have been elected President and Vice President of the United States, to extend them those best wishes, and to extend you those best wishes, as all of you work in a cause that is bigger than any man's ambition, greater than any Party. It is the cause of freedom, of justice, and peace for all mankind.

And it is in that spirit that I now declare that John F. Kennedy has been elected President of the United States, and Lyndon Johnson Vice President of the United States.

The Chair now declares the Joint Session adjourned.

Acceptance Speech, Republican National Convention, 1968

Nixon's Republican National Convention speech in 1968 marked the political return of someone who had only shortly before expressed his own sense that his career was over, and whose prevailing image was that of a two-time loser—and a sore loser at that. His unrelenting attacks on the failures of the Democratic administration would be used the soundtrack for his Fall campaign commercials, although the speech was also remembered for its uplifting concluding references to the child he thought of when he contemplated the country's future—and his own past.

* * *

Mr. Chairman, delegates to this convention, my fellow Americans:

16 years ago, I stood before this Convention to accept your nomination as the running mate of one of the greatest Americans of our time, or of any time-Dwight D. Eisenhower. 8 years ago, I had the highest honor of accepting your nomination for President of the United States. Tonight, I again proudly accept that nomination for President of the United States.

But I have news for you. This time there is a difference. This time we are going to win.

We're going to win for a number of reasons. First, a personal one. General Eisenhower, as you know, lies critically ill in the Walter Reed Hospital tonight. I have talked, however, with Mrs. Eisenhower on the telephone. She tells me that his heart is with us. And she says that there is nothing that he lives more for, and there is nothing that would lift him more, than for us to win in November. And I say let's win this one for Ike!

We're going to win because this great Convention has demonstrated to the nation that the Republican Party has the leadership, the platform and the purpose that America needs. We're going to win because you have nominated as my running mate a statesman of the first rank who will be a great campaigner, and one who is fully qualified to undertake the new responsibilities that I shall give to the next Vice President of the United States. And he is a man who fully shares my conviction and yours, that after a period of 40 years, when power has gone from the cities and the states to the government in Washington, D.C., it's time to have power go back from Washington to the states and to the cities of this country all over America.

We are going to win because at a time that America cries out for the unity that this Administration has destroyed, the Republican Party after a spirited contest for its nomination-for President and for Vice President, stands united before the nation tonight.

And I congratulate Governor Reagan. I congratulate Governor Rockefeller. I congratulate Governor Romney. I congratulate all those who have made the hard fight that they have for this nomination. And I know that you will all fight even harder for the great victor your party is going to win in November because we're going to be together in that election campaign. And a party that can unite itself will unite America.

My fellow Americans, most important, we are going to win because our cause is right. We make history tonight, not for ourselves, but for the ages. The choice we make in 1968 will determine not only the future of America, but the future of peace and freedom in the world for the last third of the 20th century. And the question that we answer tonight: can America meet this great challenge?

For a few moments, let us look at America, let us listen to America to find the answer to that question. As we look at America, we see cities enveloped in smoke and flame. We hear sirens in the night. We see Americans dying on distant battlefields abroad. 132 We see Americans hating each other; fighting each other; killing each other at home. And as we see and hear these things, millions of Americans cry out in anguish. Did we come all this way for this? Did American boys die in Normandy, and Korea, and in Valley Forge for this?

Listen to the answer to those questions. It is another voice. It is the quiet voice in the tumult and the shouting. It is the voice of the great majority of Americans, the forgotten Americans—the non-shouters, the non-demonstrators. They're not racists or sick. They are not guilty of the crime that plagues the land. They are black and they are white; they're native-born and foreign-born; they're young and they're old. They work in America's factories. They run America's businesses. They serve in government. They provide most of the soldiers who died to keep us free. They give drive to the spirit of America. They give lift to the American Dream. They give steel to the backbone of America. They are good people, they are decent people. They work, and they save, and they pay their taxes, and they care. Like Theodore Roosevelt, they know that this country will not be a good place for any of us to live in unless it is a good place for all of us to live in. This I say to you tonight is the real voice of America. In this year 1968, this is the message it will broadcast to America and to the world.

Let's never forget that despite her faults, America is a great nation. And America is great because her people are great. With Winston Churchill, we say: "We have not journeyed all this way across the centuries, across the oceans, across the mountains, across the prairies, because we are made of sugar candy."

America is in trouble today not because her people have failed, but because her leaders have failed. And what America needs are leaders to match the greatness of her people. And this great group of Americans, the forgotten Americans and others, know that the great question Americans must answer with their votes in November is this: Whether shall continue for four more years the policies of the last five years. And this is their answer and this is my answer to that question.

When the strongest nation in the world be tied down for four years in a war in Vietnam with no end in sight; when the richest nation in the world can't manage its own economy; when the nation with the greatest tradition of the rule of law is plagued by unprecedented lawlessness; when a nation that has been known for a century for equality of opportunity is torn by unprecedented racial violence; and when the President of the United States cannot travel abroad or to any major city at home without fear of a hostile demonstration, then it's time for new leadership for the United States of America.

My fellow Americans, tonight I accept the challenge and the commitment to provide that new leadership for America, and I ask you to accept it with me. And let us accept this challenge not as a grim duty but as an exciting adventure in which we are privileged to help a great nation realize its destiny. And let us begin by committing ourselves to the truth—to see it like it is, and tell it like it is; to find the truth, to speak the truth, and to live the truth. That's what we will do.

We've had enough of big promises and little action. The time has come for honest government in the United States of America. And so tonight I do not promise the millennium in the morning. I don't promise that we can eradicate poverty, and end discrimination, eliminate all danger of war in the space of four, or even eight years. But I do promise action: a new policy for peace abroad, a new policy for peace and progress and justice at home.

Look at our problems abroad. Do you realize that we face the stark truth that we are worse off in every area of the world tonight than we were when President Eisenhower left office eight years ago. That's the record. And there is only one answer to such a record of failure and that is a complete house-cleaning of those responsible for the failures of that record. The answer is a complete reappraisal of America's policies in every section of the world.

We shall begin with Vietnam. We all hope in this room that there is a chance that current negotiations may bring an honorable end to that war. And we will say nothing during this campaign that might destroy that chance. But if the war is not ended when the people choose in November, the choice will be clear. Here it is.

For four years this administration has had at its disposal the greatest military and economic advantage that one nation has ever had over another in any war in history. For four years, America's fighting men have set a record for courage and sacrifice unsurpassed in our history. For four years, this administration has had the support of the Loyal Opposition for the objective of seeking an honorable end to the struggle. Never has so much military and economic and diplomatic power been used so ineffectively. And if, after all of this time, and all of this sacrifice, and all of this support there is still no end in sight, then I say the time has come for the American people to turn to new leadership -not tied to the mistakes and the policies of the past. That is what we offer to America.

And I pledge to you tonight that the first priority, foreign policy objective of our next Administration will be to bring an honorable end to the war in Vietnam. We shall not stop there; we need a policy to prevent more Vietnams. All of America's peace-keeping institutions and all of America's foreign commitments must be re-appraised. Over the past 25 years, America has provided more than $150 billion in foreign aid to nations abroad. In Korea and now again in Vietnam, the United States furnished most of the money, most of the arms, most of the men to help the people of those countries defend themselves against aggression.

Now we're rich country. We're a strong nation. We're a populous nation. But there are 200 million Americans, and they're 2 billion people that live in the Free World. And I say the time has come for other nations in the Free World to bear their fair share of the burden of defending peace and freedom around this world.

What I call for is not a new isolationism. It is a new internationalism in which America enlists its allies and its friends around the world in those struggles in which their interest is as great as ours.

And now to the leaders of the Communist world, we say: after an era of confrontation, the time has come for an era of negotiation. Where the world's superpowers are concerned, there is no acceptable alternative to peaceful negotiation. Because this will be a period of negotiation, we shall restore the strength of America so that we shall always negotiate from strength and never from weakness.

And as we seek peace through negotiation, let our goals be made clear. We do not seek domination over any other country. We believe deeply in our ideas, but we believe they should travel on their own power and not on the power of our arms. We shall never be belligerent, but we shall be as firm in defending our system as they are in expanding theirs.

We believe this should be an era of peaceful competition, not only in the productivity of our factories but in the quality of our ideas. We extend the hand of friendship to all people, to the Russian people, to the Chinese people, to all people in the world. And we shall work toward the goal of an open world—open skies, open cities, open hearts, open minds.

The next eight years, my friends, this period in which we are entering, I think we will have the greatest opportunity for world peace but also face the greatest danger of world war of any time in our history. I believe we must have peace. I believe that we can have peace. But I do not underestimate the difficulty of this task, because, you see, the art of preserving peace is greater than that of waging war and much more demanding. But I am proud to have served in an Administration which ended one war and kept the nation out. of other wars for eight years. And it is that kind of experience and it is that kind of leadership that America needs today, and that we will give to America with your help.

And as we commit to new policies for America tonight, let me make one further pledge: For five years hardly a day has gone by when we haven't read or heard a report of the American flag being spit on; an embassy being stoned; a library being burned; or an ambassador being insulted-some place in the world. And each incident reduced respect for the United States until the ultimate insult inevitably occurred. And I say to you tonight that when respect for the United States of America falls so low that a fourth-rate military power, like North Korea, will seize an American naval vessel on the high seas, it's time for new leadership to restore respect for the United States of America.

My friends, America is a great nation. And it is time we started to act like a great nation around the world. It is ironic to note when we were a small nation—weak militarily and poor economically—America was respected. And the reason was that America stood for something more powerful than military strength or economic wealth.

The American Revolution was a shining example of freedom in action which caught the imagination of the world. And today, too often, America is an example to be avoided and not followed. A nation that can't keep the peace at home won't be trusted to keep the peace abroad. A President who isn't treated with respect at home will not be treated with respect abroad. A nation which can't manage its own economy can't tell others how to manage theirs. If we are to restore prestige and respect for America abroad, the place to begin is at home in the United States of America.

My friends, we live in an age of revolution in America and in the world. And to find the answers to our problems, let us turn to a revolution, a revolution that will never grow old, the world's greatest continuing revolution, the American Revolution.

The American Revolution was and is dedicated to progress, but our founders recognized that the first requisite of progress is order. Now, there is no quarrel between progress and order, because neither can exist without the other. So let us have order in America—not the order that suppresses dissent and discourages change, but the order which guarantees the right to dissent and provides the basis for peaceful change. And tonight, it's time for some honest talk about the problem of order in the United States.

Let us always respect, as I do, our courts and those who serve on them. But let us also recognize that some of our courts in their decisions have gone too far in weakening the peace forces as against the criminal forces in this country and we must act to restore balance. Let those who have the responsibility to enforce our laws and our judges who have the responsibility to interpret them be dedicated to the great principles of civil rights. But let them also recognize that the first civil right of every American is to be free from domestic violence, and that right must be guaranteed in this country.

And if we are to restore order and respect for law in this country there is one place we are going to begin. We are going to have a new Attorney General of the United States of America. I pledge to you that our new Attorney General will be directed by the President of the United States to launch a war against organized crime in this country. I pledge to you that the new Attorney General of the United States will be an active belligerent against the loan sharks and the numbers racketeers that rob the urban poor in our cities. I pledge to you that the new Attorney General will open a new front against the filth peddlers and the narcotics peddlers who are corrupting the lives of the children of this country.

Because, my friends, let this message come through clear from what I say tonight. Time is running out for the merchants of crime and corruption in American society. The wave of crime is not going to be the wave of the future in the United States of America. We shall re-establish freedom from fear in America so that America can take the lead in re-establishing freedom from fear in the world. And to those who say that law and order is the code word for racism, there and here, is a reply. Our goal is justice—justice for every American. If we are to have respect for law in America, we must have laws that deserve respect. Just as we cannot have progress without order, we cannot have order without progress. And so, as we commit to order tonight, let us commit to progress.

And this brings me to the clearest choice among the great issues of this campaign. For the past five years, we have been deluged by government programs for the unemployed, programs for the cities, programs for the poor. And we have reaped from these programs an ugly harvest of frustration, violence and failure across the land. And now our opponents will be offering more of the same—more billions for government jobs, government housing, government welfare. I say it is time to quit pouring billions of dollars into programs that have failed in the United States of America. To put it bluntly, we are on the wrong road and it's time to take a new road, to progress.

Again, we turn to the American Revolution for our answer. The War on Poverty didn't begin five years ago in this country. It began when this country began. It's been the most successful war on poverty in the history of nations. There is more wealth in America today, more broadly shared, than in any nation in the world. We are a great nation. And we must never forget how we became great. America is a great nation today not because of what government did for people-but because of what people did for themselves over 190 years in this country.

So it is time to apply the lessons of the American Revolution to our present problem. Let us increase the wealth of America so that we can provide more generously for the aged; and for the needy; and for all those who cannot help themselves. But for those who are able to help themselves, what we need are not more millions on welfare rolls, but more millions on payrolls in the United States of America. Instead of government jobs, and government housing, and government welfare, let government use its tax and credit policies to enlist in this battle the greatest engine of progress ever developed in the history of man—American private enterprise. Let us enlist in this great cause the millions of Americans in volunteer organizations who will bring a dedication to this task that no amount of money could ever buy. And let us build bridges, my friends, build bridges to human dignity across that gulf that separates black America from white America.

Black Americans, no more than white Americans, they do not want more government programs which perpetuate dependency. They don't want to be a colony in a nation. They want the pride, and the self-respect, and the dignity that can only come if they have an equal chance to own their own homes, to own their own businesses, to be managers and executives as well as workers, to have a piece of the action in the exciting ventures of private enterprise. And I pledge to you tonight that we shall have new programs which will provide that equal chance.

We make great history tonight. We do not fire a shot heard 'round the world, but we shall light the lamp of hope in millions of homes across this land in which there is no hope today. And that great light shining out from America will again become a beacon of hope for all those in the world who seek freedom and opportunity.

My fellow Americans, I believe that historians will recall that 1968 marked the beginning of the American generation in world history. Just to be alive in America, just to be alive at this time, is an experience unparalleled in history. Here is where the action is.

Think. 32 years from now, most of Americans living today will celebrate a new year that comes once in a thousand years. 8 years from now, in the second term of the next President, we will celebrate the 200th anniversary of the American Revolution. And by our decision in this election, we, all of us here, all of you listening on television and radio, we will determine what kind of nation America will be on its 200th birthday. We will determine what kind of a world America will live in in the year 2000.

This is the kind of a day I see for America on that glorious Fourth, eight years from now. I see a day when Americans are once again proud of their flag. When once again at home 'and abroad, it is honored as the world's greatest symbol of liberty and justice. I see a day when the President of the United States is respected and his office is honored because it is worthy of respect and worthy of honor. I see a day when every child in this land, regardless of his background, has a chance for the best education that our wisdom and schools can provide, and an equal chance to go just as high as his talents will take him. I see a day when life in rural America attracts people to the country, rather than driving them away. I see a day when we can look back on massive breakthroughs in solving the problems of slums and pollution and traffic which are choking our cities to death. I see a day when our senior citizens and millions of others, can plan for the future with the assurance that their government is not going to rob them of their savings by destroying the value of their dollars. I see a day when we will again have freedom from fear in America and freedom from fear in the world. I see a day when our nation is at peace, and the world is at peace, and everyone on Earth—those who hope, those who aspire, those who crave liberty—will look to America as the shining example of hopes realized and dreams achieved.

My fellow Americans, this is the cause I ask you to vote for. This is the cause I ask you to work for. This is the cause I ask you to commit to—not just for victory in November but beyond that, to a new administration—because the time when one man or a few leaders could save America is gone. We need tonight nothing less than the total commitment and the total mobilization of the American people if we are to succeed.

Government can pass laws, but respect for law can come only from people who take the law into their hearts and their minds, and not into their hands. Government can provide opportunity, but opportunity means nothing unless people are prepared to seize it. A president can ask for reconciliation in the racial conflict that divides Americans, but reconciliation comes only from the hearts of people.

And tonight, therefore, as we make this commitment, let us look into our hearts and let us look down into the faces of our children. Is there anything in the world that should stand in their way? None of the old hatreds mean anything when you look down into the faces of our children. In their faces is our hope, our love, and our courage.

Tonight, I see the face of a child. He lives in a great city. He's black, or he's white. He is Mexican, Italian, Polish. None of that matters. What matters—he's an American child. That child in that great city is more important than any politician's promise. He is America. He is a poet, he is a scientist, he is a great teacher, he is a proud craftsman. He is everything we ever hoped to be and everything we dare to dream to be. He sleeps the sleep of childhood, and he dreams the dreams of a child. And yet when he awakens, he awakens to a living nightmare of poverty, neglect and despair. He fails in school. He ends up on welfare. For him, the American system is one that feeds his stomach and starves his soul. It breaks his heart. And in the end, it may take his life on some distant battlefield. To millions of children in this rich land, this is their prospect of the future.

But this is only part of what I see in America. I see another child tonight. He hears the train go by at night and he dreams of faraway places where he'd like to go. It seems like an impossible dream. But he is helped on his journey through life. A father who had to go to work before he finished the sixth grade, sacrificed everything he had so that his sons could go to college. A gentle, Quaker mother, with a passionate concern for peace, quietly wept when he went to war, but she understood why he had to go. A great teacher, a remarkable football coach, an inspirational minister encouraged him on his way. A courageous wife and loyal children stood by him in victory and also in defeat. And in his chosen profession of politics, first there were scores, and then hundreds, then thousands, and finally millions worked for his success. And tonight he stands before you, nominated for President of the United States of America.

You can see why I believe so deeply in the American Dream. For most of u,s the American Revolution has been won; the American Dream has come true. And what I ask you to do tonight is to help me make that dream come true for millions to whom it's an impossible dream today.

108 years ago, the newly elected President of the United States, Abraham Lincoln, left Springfield, Illinois, never to return again. He spoke to his friends gathered at the railroad station. Listen to his words: "Today I leave you. I go to assume a greater task than devolved on General Washington. The great God which helped him must help me. Without that great assistance, I will surely fail. With it, I cannot fail."

Abraham Lincoln lost his life, but he did not fail. The next President of the United States will face challenges which in some ways will be greater than those of Washington or Lincoln. Because for the first time in our nation's history, an American President will face not only the problem of restoring peace abroad but of restoring peace at home. Without God's help, and your help, we will surely fail; but with God's help and your help, we shall surely succeed.

My fellow Americans, the long dark night for America is about to end. The time has come—the time has come—for us to leave the valley of despair and climb the mountain so that we may see the glory of the dawn, a new day for America, and a new dawn for peace and freedom in the world.

First Inaugural Address, January 20, 1969

Nixon's Inaugural Address has been noted by historians of political rhetoric as one of the best written of all Inaugural Addresses—although its immediate public impact was diluted by the anti-Vietnam demonstrations that stole the current news spotlight. It drew on draft texts by several contributors —carefully selected and woven together by Nixon over several days of isolated writing and rewriting. In directing his speech not only to the American public but also to"my fellow citizens of the world community," the speech signaled the foreign policy priorities of the new President.

* * *

Senator Dirksen, Mr. Chief Justice, Mr. Vice President, President Johnson, Vice President Humphrey, my fellow Americans-and my fellow citizens of the world community:

I ask you to share with me today the majesty of this moment. In the orderly transfer of power, we celebrate the unity that keeps us free.

Each moment in history is a fleeting time, precious and unique. But some stand out as moments of beginning, in which courses are set that shape decades or centuries. This can be such a moment. Forces now are converging that make possible, for the first time, the hope that many of man's deepest aspirations can at last be realized. The spiraling pace of change allows us to contemplate, within our own lifetime, advances that once would have taken centuries.

In throwing wide the horizons of space, we have discovered new horizons on earth. For the first time, because the people of the world want peace, and the leaders of the world are afraid of war, the times are on the side of peace.

Eight years from now, America will celebrate its 200th anniversary as a nation. And within the lifetime of most people now living, mankind will celebrate that great new year which comes only once in a thousand years – the beginning of the third millennium. What kind of a nation we will be, what kind of a world we will live in, whether we shape the future in the image of our hopes, is ours to determine by our actions and our choices.

The greatest honor history can bestow is the title of peacemaker. This honor now beckons America – the chance to help lead the world at last out of the valley of turmoil and onto that high ground of peace that man has dreamed of since the dawn of civilization. If we succeed, generations to come will say of us now living that we mastered our moment, that we helped make the world safe for mankind. This is our summons to greatness, and I believe the American people are ready to answer this call.

The second third of this century has been a time of proud achievement. We have made enormous strides in science and industry and agriculture. We have shared our wealth more broadly than ever. We have learned at last to manage a modern economy to assure its continued growth. We have given freedom new reach. We have begun to make its promise real for black as well as for white.

We see the hope of tomorrow in the youth of today. I know America's youth. I believe in them. We can be proud that they are better educated, more committed, more passionately driven by conscience than any generation in our history. No people has ever been so close to the achievement of a just and abundant society, or so possessed of the will to achieve it.

And because our strengths are so great, we can afford to appraise our weaknesses with candor and to approach them with hope.

Standing in this same place a third of a century ago, Franklin Delano Roosevelt addressed a nation ravaged by Depression and gripped in fear. He could say in surveying the Nation's troubles: "they concern, thank God, only material things." Our crisis today is in reverse. We find ourselves rich in goods but ragged in spirit; reaching with magnificent precision for the moon, but falling into raucous discord on earth. We are caught in war, wanting peace. We are torn by division, wanting unity. We see around us empty lives, wanting fulfillment. We see tasks that need doing, waiting for hands to do them. To a crisis of the spirit, we need an answer of the spirit. And to find that answer, we need only look within ourselves.

When we listen to "the better angels of our nature," we find that they celebrate the simple things, the basic things, such as goodness, decency, love, kindness. Greatness comes in simple trappings. The simple things are the ones most needed today if we are to surmount what divides us, and cement what unites us. To lower our voices would be a simple thing.

In these difficult years, America has suffered from a fever of words: from inflated rhetoric that promises more than it can deliver; from angry rhetoric that fans discontents into hatreds; from bombastic rhetoric that postures instead of persuading. We cannot learn from one another until we stop shouting at one another—until we speak quietly enough so that our words can be heard as well as our voices.

For its part, government will listen. We will strive to listen in new ways to the voices of quiet anguish, the voices that speak without words, the voices of the heart; to the injured voices, the anxious voices, the voices that have despaired of being heard. Those who have been left out, we will try to bring in. Those left behind, we will help to catch up. For all of our people, we will set as our goal the decent order that makes progress possible and our lives secure.

As we reach toward our hopes, our task is to build on what has gone before: not turning away from the old, but turning toward the new. In this past third of a century, government has passed more laws, spent more money, initiated more programs than in all our previous history. In pursuing our goals of full employment, better housing, excellence in education; in rebuilding our cities and improving our rural areas; in protecting our environment and enhancing the quality of life. In all these and more, we will and must press urgently forward. We shall plan now for the day when our wealth can be transferred from the destruction of war abroad to the urgent needs of our people at home.

The American Dream does not come to those who fall asleep. But we are approaching the limits of what government alone can do. Our greatest need now is to reach beyond government, to enlist the legions of the concerned and the committed. What has to be done, has to be done by government and people together or it will not be done at all.

The lesson of past agony is that without the people we can do nothing; with the people we can do everything. To match the magnitude of our tasks, we need the energies of our people—enlisted not only in grand enterprises, but, more importantly, in those small, splendid efforts that make headlines in the neighborhood newspaper instead of the national journal.

With these, we can build a great cathedral of the spirit, each of us raising it one stone at a time, as he reaches out to his neighbor, helping, caring, doing.

I do not offer a life of uninspiring ease. I do not call for a life of grim sacrifice. I ask you to join in a high adventure, one as rich as humanity itself, and exciting as the times we live in.

The essence of freedom is that each of us shares in the shaping of his own destiny. Until he has been part of a cause larger than himself, no man is truly whole. The way to fulfillment is in the use of our talents. We achieve nobility in the spirit that inspires that use. As we measure what can be done, we shall promise only what we know we can produce; but as we chart our goals, we shall be lifted by our dreams.

No man can be fully free while his neighbor is not. To go forward at all is to go forward together. This means black and white together, as one nation, not two.

The laws have caught up with our conscience. What remains is to give life to what is in the law : to insure at last that as all are born equal in dignity before God, all are born equal in dignity before man.

As we learn to go forward together at home, let us also seek to go forward together with all mankind. Let us take as our goal: Where peace is unknown, make it welcome; where peace is fragile, make it strong; where peace is temporary, make it permanent.

After a period of confrontation, we are entering an era of negotiation. Let all nations know that during this administration our lines of communication will be open. We seek an open world—open to ideas, open to the exchange of goods and people—a world in which no people, great or small. will live in angry isolation. We cannot expect to make everyone our friend, but we can try to make no one our enemy. Those who would be our adversaries, we invite to a peaceful competition—anot in conquering territory or extending dominion, but in enriching the life of man.

As we explore the reaches of space, let us go to the new worlds together—not as new worlds to be conquered, but as a new adventure to be shared. And with those who are willing to join, let us cooperate to reduce the burden of arms, to strengthen the structure of peace, to lift up the poor and the hungry. But to all those who would be tempted by weakness, let us leave no doubt that we will be as strong as we need to be for as long as we need to be.

Over the past 20 years, since I first came to this capital as a freshman Congressman, I have visited most of the nations of the world. I have come to know the leaders of the world, and the great forces, the hatreds, the fears that divide the world. I know that peace does not come through wishing for it—that there is no substitute for days and even years of patient and prolonged diplomacy.

I also know the people of the world. I have seen the hunger of a homeless child, the pain of a man wounded in battle, the grief of a mother who has lost her son. I know these have no ideology, no race. I know America. I know the heart of America is good. I speak from my own heart, and the heart of my country, the deep concern we have for those who suffer and those who sorrow.

I have taken an oath today in the presence of God and my countrymen to -uphold and defend the Constitution of the United States. To that oath I now add this sacred commitment: I shall consecrate my office, my energies, and all the wisdom I can summon to the cause of peace among nations. Let this message be heard by strong and weak alike.

The peace we seek—the peace we seek to win—is not victory over any other people, but the peace that comes "with healing in its wings"; with compassion for those who have suffered; with understanding for those who have opposed us; with the opportunity for all the peoples of this Earth to choose their own destiny.

Only a few short weeks ago we shared the glory of man's first sight of the world as God sees it, as a single sphere reflecting light in the darkness. As the Apollo astronauts flew over the moon's gray surface on Christmas Eve, they spoke to us of the beauty of Earth; and in that voice so clear across the lunar distance, we heard them invoke God's blessing on its goodness.

In that moment, their view from the moon moved poet Archibald MacLeish to write: "To see the Earth as it truly is, small and blue and beautiful in that eternal silence where it floats, is to see ourselves as riders on the Earth together: brothers on that bright loveliness in the eternal cold—brothers who know now they are truly brothers."

In that moment of surpassing technological triumph, men turned their thoughts toward home and humanity, seeing in that far perspective that man's destiny on Earth is not divisible; telling us that however far we reach into the cosmos, our destiny lies not in the stars but on Earth itself, in our own hands, in our own hearts.

We have endured a long night of the American spirit. But as our eyes catch the dimness of the first rays of dawn, let us not curse the remaining dark. Let us gather the light.

Our destiny offers, not the cup of despair, but the chalice of opportunity. So let us seize it, not in fear, but in gladness—and, "riders on the Earth together," let us go forward, firm in our faith, steadfast in our purpose, cautious of the dangers, but sustained by our confidence in the will of God and the promise of man.

The Silent Majority Speech

The "Silent Majority" speech, again written by Nixon himself in lonely isolation as he pondered the cresting anti-war movement, was ranked by many at the end of the twentieth century as one of the most important speeches of that period. Its public impact toward the end of his first year in the Presidency was to lift Nixon's poll ratings to new highs, building broad support for his Vietnam exit strategy—with its refusal to "bug out" and lose the war, and its removal, nonetheless, of American combat forces, while pursuing a negotiated settlement.

* * *

Good evening, my fellow Americans:

Tonight, I want to talk to you on a subject of deep concern to all Americans and to many people in all parts of the world – the war in Vietnam.

I believe that one of the reasons for the deep division about Vietnam is that many Americans have lost confidence in what their government has told them about our policy. The American people cannot and should not be asked to support a policy which involves the overriding issues of war and peace unless they know the truth about that policy.

Tonight, therefore, I would like to answer some of the questions that I know are on the minds of many of you listening to me. How and why did America get involved in Vietnam in the first place? How has this administration changed the policy of the previous administration? What has really happened in the negotiations in Paris and on the battlefront in Vietnam? What choices do we have if we are to end the war? What are the prospects for peace?

Now, let me begin by describing the situation I found when I was inaugurated on January 20. The war had been going on for 4 years. 31,000 Americans had been killed in action. The training program for the South Vietnamese was behind schedule. 540,000 Americans were in Vietm, with no plans to reduce the number. No progress had been made at the negotiations in Paris, and the United States had not put forth a comprehensive peace proposal. The war was causing deep division at home and criticism from many of our friends, as well as our enemies abroad.

In view of these circumstances there were some who urged that I end the war at once by ordering the immediate withdrawal of all American forces. From a political standpoint, this would have been a popular and easy course to follow. After all, we became involved in the war while my predecessor was in office. I could blame the defeat which would be the result of my action on him and come out as the peacemaker.

Some put it to me quite bluntly: This was the only way to avoid allowing Johnson's war to become Nixon's war. But I had a greater obligation than to think only of the years of my administration and of the next election. I had to think of the effect of my decision on the next generation and on the future of peace and freedom in American and in the world.

Let us all understand that the question before us is not whether some Americans are for peace, and some Americans are against peace. The question at issue is not whether Johnson's war becomes Nixon's war. The great question is: How can we win America's peace?

Well, let us turn now to the fundamental issue. Why and how did the United States become involved in Vietnam in the first place? 15 years ago, North Vietnam, with the logistical support of Communist China and the Soviet Union, launched a campaign to impose a Communist government on South Vietnam by instigating and supporting a revolution.

In response to the request of the government of South Vietnam, President Eisenhower sent economic aid and military equipment to assist the people of South Vietnam in their efforts to prevent a Communist takeover. 7 years ago, President Kennedy sent 16,000 military personnel to Vietnam as combat advisers. 4 years ago, President Johnson sent American combat forces to South Vietnam.

Now, many believe that President Johnson's decision to send American combat forces to South Vietnam was wrong. And many others, I among them, have been strongly critical of the way the war has been conducted. But the question facing us today is: Now that we are in the war, what is the best way to end it?

In January I could only conclude that the precipitate withdrawal of all American forces from Vietnam would be a disaster not only for South Vietnam, but for the United States and for the cause of peace. For the South Vietnamese, our precipitate withdrawal would inevitably allow the Communists to repeat the massacres which followed their takeover in the North 15 years before. They then murdered more than 50,000 people, and hundreds of thousands more died in slave labor camps.

We saw a prelude of what would happen in South Vietnam when the Communists entered the city of Hue last year. During their brief rule there, there was a bloody reign of terror in which 3,000 civilians were clubbed, shot to death, and buried in mass graves. With the sudden collapse of our support, these atrocities of Hue would become the nightmare of the entire nation, and particularly for the million and a half Catholic refugees who fled to South Vietnam when the Communists took over in the North. For the United States, this first defeat in our nation's history would result in a collapse of confidence in American leadership, not only in Asia, but throughout the world.

Three American Presidents have recognized the great stakes involved in Vietnam and understood what had to be done. In 1963, President Kennedy, with his characteristic eloquence and clarity, said, "we want to see a stable government there, carrying on a struggle to maintain its national independence. We believe strongly in that. We are not going to withdraw from that effort. In my opinion, for us to withdraw from that effort would mean a collapse not only of South Vietnam, but Southeast Asia. So we are going to stay there." President Eisenhower and President Johnson expressed the same conclusion during their terms of office.

For the future of peace, precipitate withdrawal would thus be a disaster of immense magnitude. A nation cannot remain great if it betrays its allies and lets down its friends. Our defeat and humiliation in South Vietnam, without question, would promote recklessness in the councils of those great powers who have not yet abandoned their goals of world conquest. This would spark violence wherever our commitments help maintain the peace – in the Middle East, in Berlin, eventually even in the Western Hemisphere. Ultimately, this would cost more lives. It would not bring peace; it would bring more war.

For these reasons, I rejected the recommendation that I should end the war by immediately withdrawing all of our forces. I chose instead to change American policy on both the negotiating front and battlefront.

In order to end a war fought on many fronts, I initiated a pursuit for peace on many fronts.

In a television speech on May 14, in a speech before the United Nations, and on a number of other occasions, I set forth our peace proposals in great detail. We have offered the complete withdrawal of all outside forces within 1 year. We have proposed a ceasefire under international supervision. We have offered free elections under international supervision with the Communists participating in the organization and conduct of the elections as an organized political force. And the Saigon government has pledged to accept the result of the elections.

We have not put forth our proposals on a take-it-or-leave-it basis. We have indicated that we are willing to discuss the proposals that have been put forth by the other side. We have declared that anything is negotiable, except the right of the people of South Vietnam to determine their own future. At the Paris peace conference, Ambassador Lodge has demonstrated our flexibility and good faith in 40 public meetings. Hanoi has refused even to discuss our proposals. They demand our unconditional acceptance of their terms, which are that we withdraw all American forces immediately and unconditionally, and that we overthrow the government of South Vietnam as we leave.

We have not limited our peace initiatives to public forums and public statements. I recognized, in January, that a long and bitter war like this usually cannot be settled in a public forum. That is why, in addition to the public statements and negotiations, I have explored every possible private avenue that might lead to a settlement. Tonight, I am taking the unprecedented step of disclosing to you some of our other initiatives for peace, initiatives we undertook privately and secretly because we thought we thereby might open a door which publicly would be closed. I did not wait for my inauguration to begin my quest for peace.

Soon after my election, through an individual who is directly in contact on a personal basis with the leaders of North Vietnam, I made two private offers for a rapid, comprehensive settlement. Hanoi's replies called in effect for our surrender before negotiations.

Since the Soviet Union furnishes most of the military equipment for North Vietnam, Secretary of State Rogers, my Assistant for National Security

Affairs, Dr. Kissinger, Ambassador Lodge, and I, personally have met on a number of occasions with representatives of the Soviet Government to enlist their assistance in getting meaningful negotiations started. In addition, we have had extended discussions directed toward that same end with representatives of other governments which have diplomatic relations with North Vietnam. None of these initiatives have to date produced results.

In mid-July, I became convinced that it was necessary to make a major move to break the deadlock in the Paris talks. I spoke directly in this office, where I am now sitting, with an individual who had known Ho Chi Minh on a personal basis for 25 years. Through him I sent a letter to Ho Chi Minh. I did this outside of the usual diplomatic channels with the hope that with the necessity of making statements for propaganda removed, there might be constructive progress toward bringing the war to an end. Let me read from that letter to you now.

> "Dear Mr. President:
>
> "I realize that it is difficult to communicate meaningfully across the gulf of four years of war. But precisely because of this gulf, I wanted to take this opportunity to reaffirm in all solemnity my desire to work for a just peace. I deeply believe that the war in Vietnam has gone on too long and delay in bringing it to an end can benefit no one, least of all the people of Vietnam.
>
> "The time has come to move forward at the conference table toward an early resolution of this tragic war. You will find us forthcoming and open-minded in a common effort to bring the blessings of peace to the brave people of Vietnam. Let history record that at this critical juncture, both sides turned their face toward peace rather than toward conflict and war."

I received Ho Chi Minh's reply on August 30, 3 days before his death. It simply reiterated the public position North Vietnam had taken at Paris and flatly rejected my initiative. The full text of both letters is being released to the press.

In addition to the public meetings that I have referred to, Ambassador Lodge has met with Vietnam's chief negotiator in Paris in 11 private sessions. And, we have taken other significant initiatives which must remain secret to keep open some channels of communications which may still prove to be productive.

But the effect of all the public, private, and secret negotiations which have been undertaken since the bombing halt a year ago, and since this administration came into office January 20, can be summed up in one sentence: no progress whatever has been made except agreement on the shape of the bargaining table.

Well now, who is at fault?

It has become clear that the obstacle in negotiating an end to the war is not the President of the United States. It is not the South Vietnamese government. The obstacle is the other side's absolute refusal to show the least willingness to join us in seeking a just peace. And it will not do so while it is convinced that all it has to do is to wait for our next concession, and our next concession after that one, until it gets everything it wants. There can now be no longer any questions that progress in negotiation depends only on Hanoi's deciding to negotiate, to negotiate seriously.

I realize that this report on our efforts on the diplomatic front is discouraging to the American people, but the American people are entitled to know the truth – the bad news as well as the good news – where the lives of our young men are involved.

Now let me turn, however, to a more encouraging report on another front. At the time we launched our search for peace, I recognized we might not succeed in bringing an end to the war through negotiation. I, therefore, put into effect another plan to bring peace, a plan which will bring the war to an end regardless of what happens on the negotiating front. It is in line with a major shift in U.S. foreign policy which I described in my press conference at Guam on July 25.

Let me briefly explain what has been described as the Nixon Doctrine, a policy which not only will help end the war in Vietnam, but which is an essential element of our program to prevent future Vietnams.

We Americans are a do-it-yourself people. We are an impatient people. Instead of teaching someone else to do a job, we like to do it ourselves. And this trait has been carried over into our foreign policy.

In Korea and again in Vietnam, the United States furnished most of the money, most of the arms, and most of the men to help the people of those countries defend their freedom against Communist aggression. Before any American troops were committed to Vietnam, a leader of another Asian country expressed this opinion to me when I was traveling in Asia as a private citizen. He said, "when you are trying to assist another nation defend its freedom, U.S. policy should be to help them fight the war, but not to fight the war for them."

Well, in accordance with this wise counsel, I laid down in Guam three principles as guidelines for future American policy toward Asia. First, the United States will keep all of its treaty commitments. Second, we shall provide a shield if a nuclear power threatens the freedom of a nation allied with us, or of a nation whose survival we consider vital to our security. Third, in cases involving other types of aggression, we shall furnish military and economic assistance when requested in accordance with our treaty commitments – but we shall look to the nation directly threatened to assume the primary responsibility of providing the manpower for its defense.

After I announced this policy, I found that the leaders of the Philippines, Thailand, Vietnam, South Korea, and other nations which might be threatened by Communist aggression, welcomed this new direction in American foreign policy. The defense of freedom is everybody's business, not just America's business. And it is particularly the responsibility of the people whose freedom is threatened. In the previous administration, we Americanized the war in Vietnam. In this administration, we are Vietnamizing the search for peace.

The policy of the previous administration not only resulted in our assuming the primary responsibility for fighting the war, but, even more significantly, did not adequately stress the goal of strengthening the South Vietnamese so that they could defend themselves when we left.

The Vietnamization plan was launched following Secretary Laird's visit to Vietnam in March. Under the plan, I ordered first a substantial increase in the training and equipment of South Vietnamese forces. In July, on my visit to Vietnam, I changed General Abrams' orders so that they were consistent with the objectives of our new policies. Under the new orders, the primary mission of our troops is to enable the South Vietnamese forces to assume the full responsibility for the security of South Vietnam. Our air operations have been reduced by over 20 percent.

And now we have begun to see the results of this long overdue change in American policy in Vietnam. After 5 years of Americans going into Vietnam, we are finally bringing American men home. By December 15, over 60,000 men will have been withdrawn from South Vietnam, including 20 percent of all of our combat forces. The South Vietnamese have continued to gain in strength. As a result, they have been able to take over combat responsibilities from our American troops.

Two other significant developments have occurred since this administration took office. Enemy infiltration, infiltration which is essential if they are to launch a major attack, over the last three months is less than 20 percent of what it was over the same period last year. Most important, United States casualties have declined during the last 2 months to the lowest point in 3 years.

Let me now turn to our program for the future.

We have adopted a plan which we have worked out in cooperation with the South Vietnamese for the complete withdrawal of all U.S. combat ground forces, and their replacement by South Vietnamese forces on an orderly scheduled timetable. This withdrawal will be made from strength and not from weakness. As South Vietnamese forces become stronger, the rate of American withdrawal can become greater. I have not, and do not, intend to announce the timetable for our program, and there are obvious reasons for this decision which I am sure you will understand.

As I have indicated on several occasions, the rate of withdrawal will depend on developments on three fronts. One of these is the progress which can be or might be made in the Paris talks. An announcement of a fixed timetable for our withdrawal would completely remove any incentive for the enemy to negotiate an agreement. They would simply wait until our forces had withdrawn and then move in.

The other two factors on which we will base our withdrawal decisions are the level of enemy activity and the progress of the training programs of the South Vietnamese forces. And I am glad to be able to report tonight progress on both of these fronts has been greater than we anticipated when we started the program in June for withdrawal. As a result, our timetable for withdrawal is more optimistic now than when we made our first estimates in June. Now, this clearly demonstrates why it is not wise to be frozen in on a fixed timetable. We must retain the flexibility to base each withdrawal decision on the situation as it is at that time rather than on estimates that are no longer valid.

Along with this optimistic estimate, I must in all candor leave one note of caution. If the level of enemy activity significantly increases, we might have to adjust our timetable accordingly. However, I want the record to be completely clear on one point.

At the time of the bombing halt just a year ago, there was some confusion as to whether there was an understanding on the part of the enemy that if we stopped the bombing of North Vietnam they would stop the shelling of cities in South Vietnam. I want to be sure that there is no misunderstanding on the part of the enemy with regard to our withdrawal program.

We have noted the reduced level of infiltration, the reduction of our casualties, and are basing our withdrawal decisions partially on those factors. If the level of infiltration or our casualties increase while we are trying to scale down the fighting, it will be the result of a conscious decision by the enemy.

Hanoi could make no greater mistake than to assume that an increase in violence will be to its advantage. If I conclude that increased enemy action jeopardizes our remaining forces in Vietnam, I shall not hesitate to take strong and effective measures to deal with that situation.

This is not a threat. This is a statement of policy which, as Commander in Chief of our Armed Forces, I am making in meeting my responsibility for the protection of American fighting men wherever they may be.

My fellow Americans, I am sure you can recognize from what I have said that we really only have two choices open to us if we want to end this war. I can order an immediate, precipitate withdrawal of all Americans from Vietnam without regard to the effects of that action. Or we can persist in our search for a just peace through a negotiated settlement if possible, or through continued implementation of our plan for Vietnamization if necessary, a plan in which we will withdraw all of our forces from Vietnam, on a schedule in accordance with our program, as the South Vietnamese become strong enough to defend their own freedom.

I have chosen the second course. It is not the easy way; it is the right way. It is a plan which will end the war and serve the cause of peace – not just in Vietnam, but in the Pacific and in the world.

In speaking of the consequences of a precipitate withdrawal, I mentioned that our allies would lose confidence in America. Far more dangerous, we would lose confidence in ourselves. Oh, the immediate reaction would be a sense of relief that our men were coming home. But as we saw the consequences of what we had done, inevitable remorse and divisive recrimination would scar our spirit as a people.

We have faced other crises in our history, and we have become stronger be rejecting the easy way out and taking the right way in meeting our challenges. Our greatness as a nation has been our capacity to do what has to be done when we knew our course was right.

I recognize that some of my fellow citizens disagree with the plan for peace I have chosen. Honest and patriotic Americans have reached different conclusions as to how peace should be achieved. In San Francisco a few weeks ago, I saw demonstrators carrying signs reading, "lose in Vietnam, bring the boys home." Well, one of the strengths of our free society is that any American has a right to reach that conclusion and to advocate that point of view. But as President of the United States, I would be untrue to my oath of office if I allowed the policy of this Nation to be dictated by the minority who hold the point of view and who try to impose it on the Nation by mounting demonstrations in the street.

For almost 200 years, the policy of this Nation has been made under our Constitution by those leaders in the Congress and the White House elected by all of the people. If a vocal minority, however fervent its cause, prevails over reason and the will of the majority, this nation has no future as a free society.

And now I would like to address a word, if I may, to the young people of this nation who are particularly concerned, and I understand why they are concerned about this war.

I respect your idealism. I share your concern for peace. I want peace as much as you do. There are powerful personal reasons I want to end this war. This week, I will have to sign 83 letters to mothers, fathers, wives, and loved ones of men who have given their lives for America in Vietnam. It's very little satisfaction to me that this is only one-third as many letters as I signed the first week in office. There is nothing I want more than to see the day come when I do not have to write any of those letters.

I want to end the war to save the lives of those brave young men in Vietnam. But I want to end it in a way which will increase the chance that their younger brothers and their sons will not have to fight in some future Vietnam someplace in the world.

And I want to end the war for another reason. I want to end it so that the energy and dedication of you, our young people, now too often directed into bitter hatred against those responsible for the war, can be turned to the great challenges of peace, a better life for all Americans, a better life for all people on this Earth.

I have chosen a plan for peace. I believe it will succeed. If it does not succeed, what the critics say now won't matter. If it does not succeed, what the critics say now won't matter, anything I say then won't matter.

I know it may not be fashionable to speak of patriotism or national destiny these days. But I feel it is appropriate to do so on this occasion.

200 years ago this Nation was weak and poor. But even then, America was the hope of millions in the world. Today, we have become the strongest

and richest nation in the world. And the wheel of destiny has turned so that any hope the world has for the survival of peace and freedom will be determined by whether the American people have the moral stamina and the courage to meet the challenge of free world leadership.

Let historians not record that when America was the most powerful nation in the world we passed on the other side of the road and allowed the last hopes for peace and freedom of millions of people to be suffocated by the forces of totalitarianism.

And so tonight, to you, the great silent majority of my fellow Americans, I ask for your support. I pledged in my campaign for the presidency to end the war in a way that we could win the peace. I have initiated a plan of action which will enable me to keep that pledge.

The more support I can have from the American people, the sooner that pledge can be redeemed; for the more divided we are at home, the less likely the enemy is to negotiate in Paris.

Let us be united for peace. Let us also be united against defeat. Because let us understand: North Vietnam cannot defeat or humiliate the United States. Only Americans can do that.

50 years ago, in this room and at this very desk, President Woodrow Wilson spoke words which caught the imagination of a war-weary world. He said, "this is the war to end wars." His dream for peace after World War I was shattered on the hard realities of great power politics and Woodrow Wilson died a broken man.

Tonight, I do not tell you that the war in Vietnam is the war to end war. But I do say this: I have initiated a plan which will end this war in a way that will bring us closer to that great goal to which Woodrow Wilson and every American president in our history has been dedicated, the goal of a just and lasting peace. As President, I hold the responsibility for choosing the best path to that goal and then leading the Nation along it.

I pledge to you tonight that I shall meet this responsibility, with all of the strength and wisdom I can command in accordance with your hopes, mindful of your concerns, sustained by your prayers.

Thank you and goodnight.

Address to the Nation on the Situation in Southeast Asia
President Richard M. Nixon
April 30, 1970

The "Pitiful Helpless Giant" speech and its unhappy aftermath reversed the momentum Nixon had gained in the Silent Majority speech six months earlier, polarizing the country by appearing to widen the war, and by bitterly denouncing the anti-war demonstrators. The policy it announced was a limited military action, but its rhetorical impact fostered an embattled mentality that eventually led to the fatal Watergate crisis.

* * *

Good evening, my fellow Americans:

10 days ago, in my report to the nation on Vietnam, I announced the decision to withdraw an additional 150,000 Americans from Vietnam over the next year. I said then that I was making that decision despite our concern over increased enemy activity in Laos, in Cambodia, and in South Vietnam. And at that time, I warned that if I concluded that increased enemy activity in any of these areas endangered the lives of Americans remaining in Vietnam, I would not hesitate to take strong and effective measures to deal with that situation. Despite that warning, North Vietnam has increased its military aggression in all these areas, and particularly in Cambodia.

After full consultation with the National Security Council, Ambassador Bunker, General Abrams, and my other advisers, I have concluded that the actions of the enemy in the last 10 days clearly endanger the lives of Americans who are in Vietnam now, and would constitute an unacceptable risk to those who will be there after withdrawal of another 150,000.

To protect our men who are in Vietnam and to guarantee the continued success of our withdrawal and Vietnamization programs, I have concluded that the time has come for action. Tonight, I shall describe the actions of the enemy, the actions I have ordered to deal with that situation, and the reasons for my decision.

Cambodia, a small country of seven million people, has been a neutral nation since the Geneva agreement of 1954 – an agreement, incidentally, which was signed by the government of North Vietnam. American policy since then has been to scrupulously respect the neutrality of the Cambodian people. We have maintained a skeleton diplomatic mission of fewer than 15 in Cambodia's capital, and that only since last August.

For the previous four years, from 1965 to 1969, we did not have any diplomatic mission whatever in Cambodia. And for the past five years, we have provided no military assistance whatever, and no economic assistance to Cambodia.

North Vietnam, however, has not respected that neutrality.

For the past five years – as indicated on this map that you see here – North Vietnam has occupied military sanctuaries all along the Cambodian frontier with South Vietnam. Some of these extend up to 20 miles into Cambodia. The sanctuaries are in red and, as you note, they are on both sides of the border.

They are used for hit-and-run attacks on American and South Vietnamese forces in South Vietnam. These Communist-occupied territories contain major base camps, training sites, logistics facilities, weapons and ammunition factories, airstrips, and prisoner-of-war compounds. And for five years, neither the United States nor South Vietnam has moved against these enemy sanctuaries because we did not wish to violate the territory of a neutral nation. Even after the Vietnamese Communists began to expand these sanctuaries four weeks ago, we counseled patience to our South Vietnamese allies and imposed restraints on our own commanders.

In contrast to our policy, the enemy in the past two weeks has stepped up his guerrilla actions, and he is concentrating his main forces in these sanctuaries that you see on this map, where they are building up to launch massive attacks on our forces and those of South Vietnam.

North Vietnam in the last two weeks has stripped away all pretense of respecting the sovereignty or the neutrality of Cambodia. Thousands of their soldiers are invading the country from the sanctuaries. They are encircling the capital of Phnom Penh. Coming from these sanctuaries, as you see here, they have moved into Cambodia and are encircling the capital.

Cambodia, as a result of this, has sent out a call to the United States, to a number of other nations, for assistance. Because if this enemy effort succeeds, Cambodia would become a vast enemy staging area and a springboard for attacks on South Vietnam along 600 miles of frontier – a refuge where enemy troops could return from combat without fear of retaliation. North Vietnamese men and supplies could then be poured into that country, jeopardizing not only the lives of our own men but the people of South Vietnam as well.

Now confronted with this situation, we have three options.

First, we can do nothing. Well, the ultimate result of that course of action is clear. Unless we indulge in wishful thinking, the lives of Americans remaining in Vietnam after our next withdrawal of 150,000 would be gravely threatened.

Let us go to the map again. Here is South Vietnam. Here is North Vietnam. North Vietnam already occupies this part of Laos. If North Vietnam also occupied this whole band in Cambodia, or the entire country, it would mean that South Vietnam was completely outflanked and the forces of Americans in this area, as well as the South Vietnamese, would be in an untenable military position.

Our second choice is to provide massive military assistance to Cambodia itself. Now unfortunately, while we deeply sympathize with the plight of seven million Cambodians whose country has been invaded, massive amounts of military assistance could not be rapidly and effectively utilized by the small Cambodian Army against the immediate threat. With other nations, we shall do our best to provide the small arms and other equipment which the Cambodian Army of 40,000 needs and can use for its defense. But the aid we will provide will be limited to the purpose of enabling Cambodia to defend its neutrality, and not for the purpose of making it an active belligerent on one side or the other.

Our third choice is to go to the heart of the trouble, and that means cleaning out major North Vietnamese and Vietcong occupied territories – these sanctuaries which serve as bases for attacks on both Cambodia and American and South Vietnamese forces in South Vietnam. Some of these, incidentally, are as close to Saigon as Baltimore is to Washington. This one, for example is called the Parrot's Beak. It's only 33 miles from Saigon.

Now faced with these three options, this is the decision I have made.

In cooperation with the armed forces of South Vietnam, attacks are being launched this week to clean out major enemy sanctuaries on the Cambodian-Vietnam border.

A major responsibility for the ground operations is being assumed by South Vietnamese forces. For example, the attacks in several areas, including the Parrot's Beak that I referred to a moment ago, are exclusively South Vietnamese ground operations under South Vietnamese command, with the United States providing air and logistical support.

There is one area, however, immediately above Parrot's Beak, where I have concluded that a combined American and South Vietnamese operation is necessary. Tonight, American and South Vietnamese units will attack the headquarters for the entire Communist military operation in South Vietnam. This key control center has been occupied by the North Vietnamese and Vietcong for five years, in blatant violation of Cambodia's neutrality.

This is not an invasion of Cambodia. The areas in which these attacks will be launched are completely occupied and controlled by North Vietnamese forces. Our purpose is not to occupy the areas. Once enemy forces are driven out of these sanctuaries, and once their military supplies are destroyed, we will withdraw.

These actions are in no way directed to the security interests of any nation. Any government that chooses to use these actions as a pretext for harming relations with the United States will be doing so on its own responsibility, and on its own initiative, and we will draw the appropriate conclusions.

And now let me give you the reasons for my decision.

A majority of the American people, a majority of you listening to me, are for the withdrawal of our forces from Vietnam. The action I have taken tonight is indispensable for the continuing success of that withdrawal program.

A majority of the American people want to end this war rather than to have it drag on interminably. The action I have taken tonight will serve that purpose.

A majority of the American people want to keep the casualties of our brave men in Vietnam at an absolute minimum. The action I take tonight is essential if we are to accomplish that goal.

We take this action not for the purpose of expanding the war into Cambodia but for the purpose of ending the war in Vietnam and winning the just peace we all desire. We have made – we will continue to make – every possible effort to end this war through negotiation at the conference table rather than through more fighting on the battlefield.

Let's look again at the record. We have stopped the bombing of North Vietnam. We have cut air operations by over 20 percent. We have announced withdrawal of over 250,000 of our men. We have offered to withdraw all of our men if they will withdraw theirs. We have offered to negotiate all issues with only one condition, and that is that the future of South Vietnam be determined not by North Vietnam, and not by the United States, but by the people of South Vietnam themselves.

The answer of the enemy has been intransigence at the conference table, belligerence at Hanoi, massive military aggression in Laos and Cambodia, and stepped-up attacks in South Vietnam, designed to increase American casualties.

This attitude has become intolerable. We will not react to this threat to American lives merely by plaintive diplomatic protests. If we did, the credibility of the United States would be destroyed in every area of the world where only the power of the United States deters aggression.

Tonight, I again warn the North Vietnamese that if they continue to escalate the fighting when the United States is withdrawing its forces, I shall meet my responsibility as Commander in Chief of our Armed

Forces to take the action I consider necessary to defend the security of our American men.

The action that I have announced tonight puts the leaders of North Vietnam on notice that we will be patient in working for peace, we will be conciliatory at the conference table, but we will not be humiliated. We will not be defeated. We will not allow American men by the thousands to be killed by an enemy from privileged sanctuaries.

The time came long ago to end this war through peaceful negotiations. We stand ready for those negotiations. We have made major efforts, many of which must remain secret. I say tonight: all the offers and approaches made previously remain on the conference table whenever Hanoi is ready to negotiate seriously. But if the enemy response to our most conciliatory offers for peaceful negotiation continues to be to increase its attacks and humiliate and defeat us, we shall react accordingly.

My fellow Americans, we live in an age of anarchy, both abroad and at home. We see mindless attacks on all the great institutions which have been created by free civilizations in the last 500 years. Even here in the United States, great universities are being systematically destroyed. Small nations all over the world find themselves under attack from within and from without.

If, when the chips are down, the world's most powerful nation, the United States of America, acts like a pitiful, helpless giant, the forces of totalitarianism and anarchy will threaten free nations and free institutions throughout the world.

It is not our power, but our will and character that is being tested tonight. The question all Americans must ask and answer tonight is this: does the richest and strongest nation in the history of the world have the character to meet a direct challenge by a group which rejects every effort to win a just peace, ignores our warning, tramples on solemn agreements, violates the neutrality of an unarmed people, and uses our prisoners as hostages? If we fail to meet this challenge, all other nations will be on notice that despite its overwhelming power, the United States, when a real crisis comes, will be found wanting.

During my campaign for the presidency, I pledged to bring Americans home from Vietnam; they are coming home. I promised to end this war; I shall keep that promise. I promised to win a just peace; I shall keep that promise. We shall avoid a wider war; but we are also determined to put an end to this war.

In this room, Woodrow Wilson made the great decisions which led to victory in World War I. Franklin Roosevelt made the decisions which led to our victory in World War II. Dwight D. Eisenhower made decisions which ended the war in Korea and avoided war in the Middle East. John F. Kennedy, in his finest hour, made the great decision which removed Soviet nuclear missiles from Cuba and the Western Hemisphere.

I have noted that there's been a great deal of discussion with regard to this decision that I have made, and I should point out that I do not contend that it is in the same magnitude as these decisions that I have just mentioned. But between those decisions, and this decision, there is a difference that is very fundamental. In those decisions, the American people were not assailed by counsels of doubt and defeat from some of the most widely known opinion leaders of the nation.

I have noted, for example, that a Republican Senator has said that this action I have taken means that my party has lost all chance of winning the November elections. And others are saying today that this move against enemy sanctuaries will make me a one-term President.

No one is more aware than I am of the political consequences of the action I have taken. It is tempting to take the easy political path: to blame this war on previous administrations and to bring all of our men home immediately, regardless of the consequences, even though that would mean defeat for the United States; to desert 18 million South Vietnamese people, who have put their trust in us, to expose them to the same slaughter and savagery which the leaders of North Vietnam inflicted on hundreds of thousands of North Vietnamese who chose freedom when the Communists took over North Vietnam in 1954; to get peace at any price now, even though I know that a peace of humiliation for the United States would lead to a bigger war or surrender later.

I have rejected all political considerations in making this decision. Whether my party gains in November is nothing compared to the lives of 400,000 brave Americans fighting for our country, and for the cause of peace and freedom in Vietnam. Whether I may be a one-term President is insignificant compared to whether by our failure to act in this crisis, the United States proves itself to be unworthy to lead the forces of freedom in this critical period in world history. I would rather be a one-term President, and do what I believe was right, than to be a two-term President at the cost of seeing America become a second-rate power and to see this nation accept the first defeat in its proud 190-year history.

I realize that in this war there are honest and deep differences in this country about whether we should have become involved, that there are differences as to how the war should have been conducted. But the decision I announce tonight transcends those differences, for the lives of American men are involved. The opportunity for 150,000 Americans to come home in the next 12 months is involved. The future of 18 million people in South Vietnam and 7 million people in Cambodia is involved. The possibility of winning a just peace in Vietnam and in the Pacific is at stake.

It is customary to conclude a speech from the White House by asking support for the President of the United States. Tonight, I depart from that precedent. What I ask is far more important. I ask for your support for our brave men fighting tonight halfway around the world – not for territory, not for glory, but so that their younger brothers, and their sons, and your sons can have a chance to grow up in a world of peace and freedom and justice.

Thank you and good night.

Address to the Nation on the Situation in Southeast Asia (May 8, 1972)

The "Mine the Ports" speech announced a much tougher military escalation in Vietnam, risking the all-important upcoming Moscow Arms-Control summit, and, potentially, Nixon's success in the upcoming 1972 presidential election.

But its careful, measured rhetoric helped to rally public opinion, building on the success of Nixon's recent China breakthrough and leading the way to a record landslide electoral victory.

* * *

Five weeks ago, on Easter weekend, the Communist armies of North Vietnam launched a massive invasion of South Vietnam, an invasion that was made possible by tanks, artillery, and other advanced offensive weapons supplied to Hanoi by the Soviet Union and other Communist nations. The South Vietnamese have fought bravely to repel this brutal assault. Casualties on both sides have been very high. Most tragically, there have been over 20,000 civilian casualties, including women and children, in the cities which the North Vietnamese have shelled in wanton disregard of human life.

As I announced in my report to the nation 12 days ago, the role of the United States in resisting this invasion has been limited to air and naval strikes on military targets in North and South Vietnam. As I also pointed out in that report, we have responded to North Vietnam's massive military offensive by undertaking wide-ranging, new peace efforts aimed at ending the war through negotiation.

On April 20, I sent Dr. Kissinger to Moscow for 4 days of meetings with General Secretary Brezhnev and other Soviet leaders. I instructed him to emphasize our desire for a rapid solution to the war, and our willingness to look at all possible approaches. At that time, the Soviet leaders showed an interest in bringing the war to an end on a basis just to both sides. They urged resumption of negotiations in Paris, and they indicated they would use their constructive influence.

I authorized Dr. Kissinger to meet privately with the top North Vietnamese negotiator, Lê Đức Thọ, on Tuesday, May 2 in Paris. Ambassador Porter, as you know, resumed the public peace negotiations in Paris on April 27, and again on May 4. At those meetings, both public and private, all we heard from the enemy was bombastic rhetoric and a replaying of their demands for surrender.

For example, at the May 2 secret meeting, I authorized Dr. Kissinger to talk about every conceivable avenue toward peace. The North Vietnamese flatly refused to consider any of these approaches. They refused to offer any new approach of their own. Instead, they simply read verbatim their previous public demands.

Here is what over three years of public and private negotiations with Hanoi has come down to: The United States, with the full concurrence of our South Vietnamese allies, has offered the maximum of what any President of the United States could offer:

- We have offered a de-escalation of the fighting.
- We have offered a ceasefire with a deadline for withdrawal of all American forces.
- We have offered new elections, which would be internationally supervised with the Communists participating both in the supervisory body and in the elections themselves.
- President Thieu has offered to resign one month before the elections.
- We have offered an exchange of prisoners of war in a ratio of 10 North Vietnamese prisoners for every 1 American prisoner that they release.

And North Vietnam has met every one of these offers with insolence and insult. They have flatly and arrogantly refused to negotiate an end to the war and bring peace. Their answer to every peace offer we have made has been to escalate the war.

In the two weeks alone since I offered to resume negotiations, Hanoi has launched three new military offensives in South Vietnam. In those two weeks, the risk that a Communist government may be imposed on the 17 million people of South Vietnam has increased, and the Communist offensive has now reached the point that it gravely threatens the lives of 60,000 American troops who are still in Vietnam.

There are only two issues left for us in this war. First, in the face of a massive invasion, do we stand by, jeopardize the lives of 60,000 Americans and leave the South Vietnamese to a long night of terror? This will not happen. We shall do whatever is required to safeguard American lives and American honor.

Second, in the case of complete intransigence at the conference table, do we join with our enemy to install a Communist government in South Vietnam? This too, will not happen. We will not cross the line from generosity to treachery.

We now have a clear, hard choice among three courses of action: immediate withdrawal of all American forces, continued attempts at negotiation, or decisive military action to end the war.

I know that many Americans favor the first course of action: immediate withdrawal. They believe the way to end the war is for the United States to get out, and to remove the threat to our remaining forces by simply withdrawing them. From a political standpoint, this would be a very easy choice for me to accept. After all, I did not send over one half million Americans to Vietnam. I have brought 500,000 men home from Vietnam since I took office.

But abandoning our commitment in Vietnam here and now would mean turning 17 million South Vietnamese over to Communist tyranny and terror. It would mean leaving hundreds of American prisoners in Communist hands, with no bargaining leverage to get them released. An American defeat in Vietnam would encourage this kind of aggression all over the world; aggression in which smaller nations, armed by their major allies, could be tempted to attack neighboring nations at will – in the Mideast, in Europe, and other areas. World peace would be in grave jeopardy.

The second course of action is to keep on trying to negotiate a settlement. Now, this is the course we have preferred from the beginning, and we shall continue to pursue it. We want to negotiate. But we have made every reasonable offer and tried every possible path for ending this war at the conference table. The problem is, as you all know, it takes two to negotiate. And now, as throughout the past four years, the North Vietnamese arrogantly refuse to negotiate anything but an imposition, an ultimatum, that the United States impose a Communist regime on 17 million people in South Vietnam who do not want a Communist government.

It's plain then that what appears to be a choice among three courses of action for the United States is really no choice at all. The killing in this tragic war must stop. By simply getting out, we would only worsen the bloodshed. By relying solely on negotiations, we would give an intransigent enemy the time he needs to press his aggression on the battlefield.

There's only one way to stop the killing. That is, to keep the weapons of war out of the hands of the international outlaws of North Vietnam.

Throughout the war in Vietnam, the United States has exercised a degree of restraint unprecedented in the annals of war. That was our responsibility as a great nation, a nation which is interested – and we can be proud of this, as Americans, as America has always been – in peace, not in conquest.

However, when the enemy abandons all restraint, throws its whole army into battle in the territory of its neighbor, refuses to negotiate, we simply face a new situation. In these circumstances, with 60,000 Americans threatened, any president who failed to act decisively would have betrayed the trust of his country and betrayed the cause of world peace.

I therefore concluded that Hanoi must be denied the weapons and supplies it needs to continue the aggression. In full coordination with the Republic of Vietnam, I have ordered the following measures which are being implemented as I am speaking to you:

- All entrances to North Vietnamese ports will be mined to prevent access to these ports and North Vietnamese naval operations from these ports.
- The United States forces have been directed to take appropriate measures within the internal and claimed territorial waters of North Vietnam to interdict the delivery of any supplies.
- Rail and all other communications will be cut off to the maximum extent possible.
- Air and naval strikes against military targets in North Vietnam will continue.

These actions are not directed against any other nation. Countries with ships presently in North Vietnamese ports have already been notified that their ships will have three daylight periods to leave in safety. After that time, the mines will become active, and any ships attempting to leave or enter these ports will do so at their own risk.

These actions I have ordered will cease when the following conditions are met. First, all American prisoners of war must be returned. Second, there must be an internationally supervised ceasefire throughout Indochina. Once prisoners of war are released, once the internationally supervised ceasefire has begun, we will stop all acts of force throughout Indochina. And at that time, we will proceed with a complete withdrawal of all American forces from Vietnam within four months.

Now these terms are generous terms. They are terms which would not require surrender and humiliation on the part of anybody. They would permit the United States to withdraw with honor. They would end the killing. They would bring our POWs home. They would allow negotiations on a political settlement between the Vietnamese themselves. They would permit all the nations which have suffered in this long war – Cambodia, Laos, North Vietnam, South Vietnam – to turn at last to the urgent works of healing and of peace. They deserve immediate acceptance by North Vietnam.

It is appropriate to conclude my remarks tonight with some comments directed individually to each of the major parties involved in the continuing tragedy of the Vietnam War.

First, to the leaders of Hanoi: your people have already suffered too much in your pursuit of conquest. Do not compound their agony with continued arrogance. Choose instead the path of a peace that redeems your sacrifices, guarantees true independence for your country, and ushers in an era of reconciliation.

To the people of South Vietnam: you shall continue to have our firm support in your resistance against aggression. It is your spirit that will determine the outcome of the battle. It is your will that will shape the future of your country.

To other nations, especially those which are allied with North Vietnam: the actions I have announced tonight are not directed against you. Their sole purpose is to protect the lives of 60,000 Americans who would be gravely endangered in the event that the Communist offensive continues to roll forward, and to prevent the imposition of a Communist government by brutal aggression upon 17 million people.

I particularly direct my comments tonight to the Soviet Union. We respect the Soviet Union as a great power. We recognize the right of the Soviet Union to defend its interests when they are threatened. The Soviet Union, in turn, must recognize our right to defend our interests. No Soviet soldiers are threatened in Vietnam. 60,000 Americans are threatened. We expect you to help your allies, and you cannot expect us to do other than to continue to help our allies. But let us, and let all great powers, help our allies only for the purpose of their defense, not for the purpose of launching invasions against their neighbors. Otherwise, the cause of peace, the cause in which we both have so great a stake, will be seriously jeopardized.

Our two nations have made significant progress in our negotiations in recent months. We are near major agreements on nuclear arms limitation, on trade, on a host of other issues. Let us not slide back toward the dark shadows of a previous age. We do not ask you to sacrifice your principles or your friends; but neither should you permit Hanoi's intransigence to blot out the prospects we together have so patiently prepared.

We, the United States and the Soviet Union, are on the threshold of a new relationship that can serve not only the interests of our two countries, but the cause of world peace. We are prepared to continue to build this relationship. The responsibility is yours if we fail to do so.

And finally, may I say to the American people: I ask you for the same strong support you have always given your president in difficult moments. It is you, most of all, that the world will be watching. I know how much you want to end this war. I know how much you want to bring our men home. And I think you know from all that I have said and done these past three and a half years, how much I too want to end the war, to bring our men home.

You want peace. I want peace. But you also want honor and not defeat. You want a genuine peace, not a peace that is merely a prelude to another war. At this moment, we must stand together in purpose and resolve.

As so often in the past, we Americans did not choose to resort to war – it has been forced upon us by an enemy that has shown utter contempt toward every overture we have made for peace. And that is why, my fellow Americans, tonight, I ask for your support of this decision, a decision which has only one purpose: not to expand the war, not to escalate the war, but to end this war and to win the kind of peace that will last. With God's help, with your support, we will accomplish that great goal.

Thank you and goodnight.

The Resignation Speech

Good evening.

This is the 37th time I have spoken to you from this office, where so many decisions have been made that shaped the history of this nation. Each time, I have done so to discuss with you some matter that I believe affected the national interest.

In all the decisions I have made in my public life, I have always tried to do what was best for the nation. Throughout the long and difficult period of Watergate, I have felt it was my duty to persevere, to make every possible effort to complete the term of office to which you elected me.

In the past few days, however, it has become evident to me that I no longer have a strong enough political base in the Congress to justify continuing that effort. As long as there was such a base, I felt strongly that it was necessary to see the constitutional process through to its conclusion, that to do otherwise would be unfaithful to the spirit of that deliberately difficult process, and a dangerously destabilizing precedent for the future.

But with the disappearance of that base, I now believe that the constitutional purpose has been served, and there is no longer a need for the process to be prolonged.

I would have preferred to carry through to the finish whatever the personal agony it would have involved, and my family unanimously urged me to do so. But the interest of the nation must always come before any personal considerations.

From the discussions I have had with Congressional and other leaders, I have concluded that because of the Watergate matter, I might not have the support of the Congress that I would consider necessary to back the very difficult decisions and carry out the duties of this office in the way the interests of the nation would require.

I have never been a quitter. To leave office before my term is completed is abhorrent to every instinct in my body. But as President, I must put the interests of America first. America needs a full-time President and a full-time Congress, particularly at this time with problems we face at home and abroad. To continue to fight through the months ahead for my personal vindication would almost totally absorb the time and attention of both the President and the Congress in a period when our entire focus should be on the great issues of peace abroad and prosperity without inflation at home.

Therefore, I shall resign the Presidency effective at noon tomorrow. Vice President Ford will be sworn in as President at that hour in this office.

As I recall the high hopes for America with which we began this second term, I feel a great sadness that I will not be here in this office working on your behalf to achieve those hopes in the next two and a half years. But in turning over direction of the government to Vice President Ford, I know, as I told the nation when I nominated him for that office 10 months ago, that the leadership of America will be in good hands.

In passing this office to the Vice President, I also do so with the profound sense of the weight of responsibility that will fall on his shoulders tomorrow; and therefore, of the understanding, the patience, the cooperation he will need from all Americans. As he assumes that responsibility, he will deserve the help and the support of all of us.

As we look to the future, the first essential is to begin healing the wounds of this nation, to put the bitterness and divisions of the recent past behind us, and to rediscover those shared ideals that lie at the heart of our strength and unity as a great and as a free people. By taking this action, I hope that I will have hastened the start of that process of healing which is so desperately needed in America.

I regret deeply any injuries that may have been done in the course of the events that led to this decision. I would say only that if some of my judgments were wrong – and some were wrong – they were made in what I believed at the time to be the best interest of the nation.

To those who have stood with me during these past difficult months – to my family, my friends, to many others who joined in supporting my cause because they believed it was right – I will be eternally grateful for your support. And to those who have not felt able to give me your support, let me say I leave with no bitterness toward those who have opposed me, because all of us, in the final analysis, have been concerned with the good of the country, however our judgments might differ. So let us all now join together in affirming that common commitment, and in helping our new President succeed for the benefit of all Americans.

I shall leave this office with regret at not completing my term, but with gratitude for the privilege of serving as your President for the past five and a half years. These years have been a momentous time in the history of our nation and the world. They have been a time of achievement in which we can all be proud, achievements that represent the shared efforts of the administration, the Congress, and the people. But the challenges ahead are equally great, and they too will require the support and the efforts of the Congress and the people, working in cooperation with the new administration.

We have ended America's longest war, but in the work of securing a lasting peace in the world, the goals ahead are even more far-reaching and more difficult. We must complete a structure of peace so that it will be said of this generation – our generation – of Americans, by the people of all nations, not only that we ended one war, but that we prevented future wars.

We have unlocked the doors that for a quarter of a century stood between the United States and the People's Republic of China. We must now ensure that the one quarter of the world's people who live in the People's Republic of China will be, and remain, not our enemies, but our friends.

In the Middle East, 100 million people in the Arab countries, many of whom have considered us their enemy for nearly 20 years, now look on us as their friends. We must continue to build on that friendship so that peace can settle at last over the Middle East, and so that the cradle of civilization will not become its grave.

Together with the Soviet Union, we have made the crucial breakthroughs that have begun the process of limiting nuclear arms. But we must set as our goal not just limiting, but reducing, and finally destroying, these terrible weapons so that they cannot destroy civilization, and so that the threat of nuclear war will no longer hang over the world and the people.

We have opened the new relation with the Soviet Union. We must continue to develop and expand that new relationship so that the two strongest nations of the world will live together in cooperation rather than confrontation.

Around the world – in Asia, in Africa, in Latin America, in the Middle East – there are millions of people who live in terrible poverty, even starvation. We must keep as our goal turning away from production for war and expanding production for peace, so that people everywhere on this earth can at last look forward in their children's time, if not in our own time, to having the necessities for a decent life.

Here in America, we are fortunate that most of our people have not only the blessings of liberty, but also the means to live full and good and, by the world's standards, even abundant lives. We must press on, however, toward a goal not only of more and better jobs but of full opportunity for every American; and of what we are striving so hard right now to achieve, prosperity without inflation.

For more than a quarter of a century in public life, I have shared in the turbulent history of this era. I have fought for what I believed in. I have tried, to the best of my ability, to discharge those duties and meet those responsibilities that were entrusted to me.

Sometimes I have succeeded, and sometimes I have failed. But always I have taken heart from what Theodore Roosevelt once said about "the man in the arena, whose face is marred by dust and sweat and blood, who strives valiantly, who errs and comes short again and again because there is not effort without error and shortcoming, but who does actually strive to do the deed, who knows the great enthusiasms, the great devotions, who spends himself in a worthy cause, who at the best, knows in the end the triumphs of high achievements, and who at the worst, if he fails, at least fails while daring greatly."

I pledge to you tonight that as long as I have a breath of life in my body, I shall continue in that spirit. I shall continue to work for the great causes to which I have been dedicated throughout my years as a Congressman, a Senator, a Vice President, and President – the cause of peace, not just for America but among all nations, prosperity, justice, and opportunity for all of our people.

There is one cause above all to which I have been devoted, and to which I shall always be devoted for as long as I live.

When I first took the oath of office as President five and a half years ago, I made this sacred commitment, to "consecrate my office, my energies, and all the wisdom I can summon to the cause of peace among nations."

I have done my very best, in all of the days since, to be true to that pledge. As a result of these efforts, I am confident that the world is a safer place today, not only for the people of America but for the people of all nations, and that all of our children have a better chance than before of living in peace rather than dying in war.

This, more than anything, is what I hoped to achieve when I sought the presidency. This, more than anything, is what I hope will be my legacy to you, to our country, as I leave the presidency.

To have served in this office is to have felt a very personal sense of kinship with each and every American. In leaving it, I do so with this prayer: May God's grace be with you in all the days ahead.

* * *

The Final Speech to the Staff

Well, members of the Cabinet, members of the White House Staff, all of our friends here:

I think the record should show that this is one of those spontaneous things that we always arrange whenever the President comes in to speak, and it will be so reported in the press, and we don't mind because they've got to call it as they see it. But on our part, believe me, it is spontaneous. You are here to say goodbye to us, and we don't have a good word for it in English. The best is "*au revoir*," "we'll see you again."

I just met with the members of the White House staff, you know, those that serve here in the White House, day in and day out. And I asked them to do what I ask all of you to do to the extent that you can and are, of course, are requested to do so: to serve our next President as you have served me and previous presidents because many of you have been here for many years with devotion and dedication, because this Office, great as it is, can only be as great as the men and women who work for and with the President.

This House, for example – I was thinking of it as we walked down this hall, and I was comparing it to some of the great Houses of the world that I've been in. This isn't the biggest House: many and most, in even smaller countries are much bigger. This isn't the finest House: many in Europe, particularly, and in China, Asia, have paintings of great, great value, things that we just don't have here, and probably will never have until we are a thousand years old or older.

But this is the best House. It's the best House because it has something far more important than numbers of people who serve, far more important than numbers of rooms or how big it is, far more important than numbers of magnificent pieces of art. This House has a great heart, and that heart comes from those who serve.

I was rather sorry they didn't come down; we said goodbye to them upstairs. But they're really great. And I recall after so many times I have made speeches, and some of them pretty tough, yet, I always come back, or after a hard day – and my days usually have run rather long – I'd always get a lift from them, because I might be a little down, but they always smiled. And so it is with you.

I look around here, and I see so many in this staff that, you know, I should have been by your offices and shaken hands, and I'd loved to have talked to you and found out how to run the world. Everybody wants to tell the President what to do, and boy he needs to be told many times, but I just haven't had the time. But I want to know – I want you to know that each and every one of you, I know, is indispensable to this government.

I'm proud of this cabinet. I'm proud of our – all the members who have served in our cabinet. I'm proud of our sub-cabinet. I am proud of our White House staff. As I pointed out last night, I'm sure we've done some things wrong in this Administration, and the top man always takes the responsibility, and I've never ducked it.

But I want to say one thing. We can be proud of it – five and a half years. No man or no woman, came into this administration and left it with more of this world's goods than when he came in. No man or no woman ever profited at the public expense or the public till. That tells something about you. Mistakes, yes; but for personal gain, never. You did what you believed in. Sometimes right, sometimes wrong. And I only wish that I were a – a wealthy man. At the present time I've got to find a way to pay my taxes – and if I were, I'd like to recompense you for the sacrifices that all of you have made to serve in government.

But, you are getting something in government – and I want you to tell this to your children, and I hope the nation's children will hear it, too – something in government service that is far more important than money. It's a cause bigger than yourself. It's the cause of making this the greatest nation in the world, the leader of the world, because without our leadership the world will know nothing but war, possibly starvation, or worse in the years ahead. With our leadership, it will know peace; it will know plenty.

We have been generous, and we will be more generous in the future as we are able to. But most important, we must be strong here, strong in our hearts, strong in our souls, strong in our belief, and strong in our willingness to sacrifice, as you have been willing to sacrifice, in a pecuniary way, to serve in government.

Something else I'd like for you to tell your young people. You know, people often come in and say, "what will I tell my kids?" you know? They look at government and – sort of a rugged life, and they see the mistakes that are made. They get the impression that everybody is here for the purpose of feathering his nest. That's why I made this earlier point – not in this administration, not one single man or woman. And I say to them, "there are many fine careers. This country needs good farmers, good businessmen, good plumbers, good carpenters."

I remember my old man. I think that they would have called him sort of – a sort of little man, a common man. He didn't consider himself that way. You know what he was? He was a streetcar motorman first, and then he was a farmer, and then he had a lemon ranch. It was the poorest lemon ranch in California, I can assure you. He sold it before they found oil on it. And then he was a grocer. But he was a great man because he did his job, and every job counts up to the hilt, regardless of what happened.

Nobody will ever write a book, probably, about my mother. Well, I guess all of you would say this about your mother: my mother was a saint. And I think of her, two boys dying of tuberculosis, nursing four others in order that she could take care of my older brother for three years in Arizona, and seeing each of them die. And when they died, it was like one of her own. Yes, she will have no books written about her. But she was a saint.

Now, however, we look to the future. Had a little quote in the speech last night[1] from T.R. [Theodore Roosevelt]. As you know, I kind of like to read books – I'm not educated, but I do read books – and the T.R. quote was a pretty good one. Here is another one I found as I was reading – my last night in the White House – and this quote is about a young man. He was a young lawyer in New York. He'd married a beautiful girl, and they had a lovely daughter. And then suddenly she died, and this is what he wrote. This was in his diary. He said:

> "She was beautiful in face and form, and lovelier still in spirit. As a flower she grew, and as a fair young flower she died. Her life had been always in the sunshine; there had never come to her a single great sorrow; none ever knew her who did not love and revere her for her bright and sunny temper, and her saintly unselfishness. Fair, pure, and joyous as a maiden; loving, tender, and happy. As a young wife; when she had just become a mother, when her life seemed to be just begun, and then the years seemed so bright before her – then by a strange and terrible fate death came to her. And when my heart's dearest died – the light went from my life forever."

That was T.R. in his twenties. He thought the light had gone from his life forever – but he went on. And he not only became President but, as an ex-President, he served his country always in the arena. Tempestuous, strong, sometimes wrong, sometimes right, but he was a man. And as I leave, let me say, that's an example I think all of us should remember.

We think sometimes when things happen that don't go the right way, we think that when you don't pass the bar exam the first time – I happened to, but I was just lucky. I mean, my writing was so poor the bar examiner said, "we've just gotta let the guy through." We think that when someone dear to us dies, we think that when we lose an election, we think that when we suffer a defeat, that all is ended. We think, as T.R. said, that the light had left his life forever.

Not true. It's only a beginning – always. The young must know it; the old must know it. It must always sustain us because the greatness comes not when things go always good for you, but the greatness comes and you are really tested, when you take some knocks, some disappointments, when sadness comes, because only if you've been in the deepest valley can you ever know how magnificent it is to be on the highest mountain.

And so, I say to you on this occasion, we leave, we leave proud of the people who have stood by us and worked for us and served this country. We want you to be proud of what you've done. We want you to continue to serve in government, if that is your wish. Always give your best, never get discouraged, never be petty. Always remember: others may hate you, but those who hate you don't win unless you hate them – and then you destroy yourself.

And so we leave with high hopes, in good spirit, and with deep humility, and with very much gratefulness in our hearts. I can only say to each and every one of you: we come from many faiths, we pray perhaps to different gods – but really the same God in a sense – but I want to say for each and every one of you, not only will we always remember you, not only will we always be grateful to you, but always you will be in our hearts and you will be in our prayers

Thank you very much.

ACKNOWLEDGEMENTS AND SOURCE NOTES FOR NIXON'S ELUSIVE TOTALITY

In thinking about the "sources" who have helped me develop this book, I think initially about those who have been so supportive in the final drafting process, including my wife, Berna, and our children Charley and David. Their patience, enthusiasm, and encouragement were essential to its progress and its completion and I am deeply grateful for the role they played and the good spirit with which they played it. The same thing is true for my colleagues and students at the George Washington University, as well as other collaborators, editors,and designers who have seen this project through to completion, especially publisher Nell Minow and editor Jeremy Fassler

Friends and colleagues with whom I shared in working directly for Richard Nixon, in campaigns, at the White House and in his post-resignation years, have been central, of course, in shaping my impressions about the President--at the time we worked with him and since. I extend my deepest gratitude to them and to many others who may not be cited in this book but whose advice and encouragement have also contributed significantly to the project.

* * *

The author's personal papers, including his White House files from his time in the Nixon administration (1969-1974) have been archived at the Northwestern University Library in Evanston, Illinois. Other critical records can be found at the Richard Nixon Presidential Library and Museum in Yorba Linda, California.

Essential reading, of course, also includes Nixon's own books: his memoirs, RN (1978), his later personal essays, In the Arena (1990), his first book, Six Crises (1961) and a series of policy-oriented books written after he left the presidency.

Among the most helpful of the books that I have used for my Nixon-related classes and in preparing this volume have been David Greenberg, Nixon's Shadow: The History of an Image (2003); Evan Thomas, Being Nixon: A Man Divided (2015); and Richard Nixon, The Life (2017) by John A. Farrell. Although it is now out-of-print, one of the best accounts of Nixon's early years is found in Jonathan Aitken's Nixon: A Life (1993). Important insights into Nixon's emotional life are found in One Lost Soul: Richard Nixon's Search for Salvation by Daniel Silliman (2024). The Nixon-related discussion in Henry Kissinger's Study of Leadership (2022) provides valuable insights into Nixon's thought processes, especially regarding his pathbreaking role on the international scene.

A close, day by day look at Nixon's Presidency is found in Richard Reeves, President Nixon. Alone in the White House (2001), which captures the reality of how a mingling of varied challenges and opportunities will simultaneously crowd their way onto the President's agenda. The Presidency of Richard Nixon (1999) by Melvin Small provides a full historical run-down Nixon's presidential record.

Three very important new histories of the Nixon administration appeared in 2021. They include: The Last Liberal Republican: An Insider's Perspective on Nixon's Surprising Social Policy by John R. Price; King Richard: Nixon and Watergate—An American Tragedy by Michael Dobbs; and

Three Days at Camp David, How a Secret Meeting in 1971 Transformed the Global Economy by Jeffrey Garton.

In addition to the materials listed above, other useful works that have come out over time include Nixon Agonistes (1970) by Gary Wills, an early three volume biography by Stephen Ambrose, Nixon (1987–1991), Richard Nixon: A Psychobiography by Volkan, N. Itzkowitz, and A. Dod (1997); Roger Morris's Richard Milhous Nixon: The Rise of an American Politician (1989), Tom Wicker's One of Us (1991), Richard Parmet's Richard Nixon and His America (1990); Christopher Matthews' Kennedy and Nixon (1996). Three notable books appeared in 2007: Conrad Black's, Nixon, A Life in Full, Elizabeth Drew's Richard M. Nixon, and Robert Dallek's, Nixon and Kissinger: Partners in Power.

More recent titles include Reinventing Richard Nixon: A Cultural History of an American Obsession (2008) by Daniel Frick; Poisoning the Press (2010) by Mark Feldstein; A Companion to Richard M. Nixon (2011), which is a series of scholarly essays edited by Melvin Small; a novelistic treatment by Thomas Mallon, Watergate (2012); Jeffrey Frank's Ike and Dick, Portrait of a Strange Political Marriage (2013); Kevin Mattson's Just Plain Dick: Richard Nixon's Checkers Speech and the "Rocking, Socking" Election of 1952 (2012); and The Mysterious Mr. Nixon: The Life and Time of Washington's Most Private First Lady, by Heath Hardage Lee (2024). See also: Ken Khachigian's Behind Closed Doors: In the Room with Reagan and Nixon (2024).

An additional flood of publications accompanied the 100th anniversary of Nixon's birth in 2013—and the 40th anniversary of his resignation in 2014. They include: The Nixon Defense: What He Knew and When He Knew It, by John Dean; The Greatest Comeback: How Richard Nixon Rose From Defeat to Create the New Majority by Patrick J. Buchanan; The Invisible Bridge: The Fall of Nixon and The Rise of Reagan, by Rick Perlstein; Richard Nixon and The Vietnam War: The End of the American Century by David Schmitz; Resilient America: Electing Nixon in 1968,

Channeling Dissent, and Dividing Government by Michael Nelson; Pat and Dick: The Nixons, Intimate Portrait of a Marriage, by Will Swift; and *Washington Journal: Reporting Watergate and Nixon's Downfall*, the republication of a 1975 book by Elizabeth Drew. See also The Professor and the President: Daniel Patrick Moynihan in the Nixon White House, by Steven Hess.
All of this in 2013 and 2014!

Plus, even more in 2015 and 2016: Two enormous volumes entitled The Nixon Tapes, by Douglas Brinkley and Luke Nichter; Ken Hughes, Fatal Politics: The Nixon Tapes, the Vietnam War, and the Casualties of Reelection; William Burr and Jeffrey Kimball, Nixon's Nuclear Specter: The Secret Alert of 1969, Madman Diplomacy, and the Vietnam War; Tim Weiner's "decidedly hostile" One Man Against the World, The Tragedy of Richard Nixon; the more "judicious" Evan Thomas study cited above; Irwin Gellman, The President and the Apprentice: Eisenhower and Nixon, 1952-1961; and Douglas Schoen, The Nixon Effect: How Richard Nixon's Presidency Fundamentally Changed American Politics (among others). Pat Buchanan added a book entitled Nixon's White House Wars to the list in 2017. The Contender: Richard Nixon, the Congress Years, 1946-1952, by Irwin Gellman also came out in 2017, and another in Gellman's series of deeply researched Nixon books appeared in 2021 entitled Campaign of the Century, Kennedy, Nixon and the Election of 1960.

An interesting book drawing on Nixon's White House tape recordings was published in 2018 and is called They Said No to Nixon: Republicans Who Stood Up to the President's Abuses of Power by Michael Koncewicz. Haig's Coup (2019) is a highly controversial account of Nixon's resignation by Ray Locker. Two recent books on Nixon's post-resignation life are Kasey S. Pipes, After the Fall: The Remarkable Comeback of Richard Nixon (2019) and Michael A Endicott, After Watergate: The Renaissance of Richard Nixon (2018). Nixon Rebuilds: from Defeat to the White House, 1962-1968 by J.D. Briley appeared in 2021. Dwight Chapin's personal memoir entitled The President's Man was published in 2022.

Other significant books, such as Bob Woodward and Carl Bernstein's Watergate accounts – All the President's Men (1974) and The Final Days (1976) —provide essential background on the Nixon era. Oliver Stone's highly controversial film and often unreliable film called *Nixon* is another example of how mythologies about the former President can influence public memory. Observers have suggested that only Washington and Lincoln, among American Presidents, have been the subject of more film projects than Richard Nixon.

Particularly valuable in-depth resources include the long post-resignation interviews that Nixon did with David Frost on national television and with Frank Gannon (the aide who helped him with his memoirs, and who is closely associated with the Richard Nixon Presidential Library and Museum.) The original telecasts of the Frost interviews in the spring of 1977 were edited down to six hours, spread over four sessions, although the full interviews were more than four times that length. The full Gannon interviews, which took place in 1983, run for some 30 hours.